Email Marketing Mastery

Accelerate Your Business Using Email Marketing

Mitch Tarr

Email Marketing Mastery
Accelerate Your Business Using Email Marketing

©2018 Mitch Tarr

ISBN-13: 978-1981286386
ISBN-10: 1981286381

Publishing by ZinMarketing Inc.

TABLE OF CONTENTS

INTRO

In 2003, when I got my first Constant Contact account, the world of email marketing was both simple and mystifying at the same time.

The tools to do email marketing were cumbersome and hard to manipulate but you could reach your readers without too much fanfare — if you followed good practices.

Even in those days, spam was a problem and legislators were working hard on how to make the CAN-SPAM act a reality.

Now as I write this you hear Constant Contact ads constantly on NPR and you can't visit many sites on the web and not see banner ads for email marketing.

But has much changed?

Senders, software, and spammers are more sophisticated, but the fundamentals of email marketing haven't changed.

The wave of social media strategies that swept the web first promised to push email aside but more recently have realized that email is indispensable in the modern web. I remember the day when the Facebook COO decreed that 'email is dead.' In reality, she meant, "we don't know how to capitalize on email."

Today email users are pretty clear on one thing... spam is spam if they say it is. That's the only definition that matters.

What does this all mean to you as a 'typical' small business owner, entrepreneur, professional, e-commerce provider, or online marketer?

It means the fundamentals work. Learn the fundamentals and you'll be able to keep focused on good marketing, which will get you way further ahead than if you look for the latest hacks and next piece of fancy software.

This book is designed to teach you the IMPORTANT parts of email marketing. The things to stay focused on. Do these things well and you'll get good results.

After running over 3,400 campaigns in the past 10 years I've learned by experience and testing what works and what does not.

You can skip the time it takes to learn the hard way. I'll share my experience with you here and lay it out, so you can get the best results possible with the least amount of effort.

If you're a skimmer or an ADHD entrepreneur, read the FAST 5. If you don't do anything else but these 5 things, you're going to get better results.

Perhaps remarkably better.

To a Great Year.

— Mitch Tarr ZinMarketing Inc.

The Myth of Email Marketing

O kay, you've made the decision to get serious about email marketing and you might be asking yourself "Where do I start?"

That is the right question.

Except you might be wondering which software is the BEST for deliverability, what template will work best for your industry, or what you should say in your newsletter.

You're getting WAY ahead of yourself. You need to take a step back. Way back.

And ask yourself this first important question.

"What do I want email marketing to do for my business?"

The way we look at it. Email marketing is just a tool... a tactic, if you will.

As such, that means that email marketing can be used for a *wide variety* of uses.

You can use email campaigns to:

- increase customer loyalty
- increase reorder rates
- generate advertising revenue
- generate leads
- generate sales
- sell out old inventory
- fill events
- pre-sell into a trade show
- support customer service
- launch new products
- tackle reducing cart abandonments

- support direct mail campaigns
- lead or enhance social media campaigns
- confirm transactions and shipping notices
- deliver a monthly newsletter
- create massive upsell revenue
- convert leads to prospects to customers
- support your sales team
- solicit product development feedback
- protect your blue-chip customers
- run marketing or service surveys

See?

The list goes on and on.

That's why to have to step back and create an email strategy.

It all starts with good strategy. You really have to know what you want email to do for your company. This is the first place things break down. Mostly you don't know what email is fully capable of and as a result you tend to underutilize this powerful channel.

Or you don't even think about it and just set up a newsletter and then feel like email doesn't work for YOUR business.

Make sure email marketing is supportive of your overall business goals. You want a campaign to do lead generation? Good. You want a campaign to increase customer loyalty? Fine. Just don't try to make one email do both.

That's one of the most common mistakes. Looking at the world through the lens of the email.

When you're looking at your email strategy, you'll want to make email work for you in as many areas as possible and because you can't make one email (like a newsletter) do EVERYTHING you have to make each email do one SPECIFIC thing.

Use this exercise to organize your email campaigns.

Ask these three questions each time you imagine creating an email campaign.

1. Who is intended to get this email?

2. How does this support my current marketing or business plans?

3. What action do I want my readers to take?

Once you have a list of ALL the possible way you can use email (see examples above) you can examine each one by asking these three questions.

Soon you'll find email DOES work for your business and you WILL get better results and you'll probably find you are just scratching the surface of how to make the most effective use of email for your business.

ABOUT MITCH

EARLY LESSONS FROM IBM AND ORACLE

My first job in the corporate world was working as a Marketing Representative at IBM. Sales, in other words. No need to go into my career at Big Blue, other than to say this is a company that believes in training their employees and had very high expectations of excellence.

One of my early tasks as a salesman was to do lead generation in my territory. In those days, there was no digital marketing or electronic communications. What we did have were a typing pool and a phone book.

We used to take the phone book, find the contact name for the President or Owner, and send them a personal letter of introduction. Which, we then followed up with a phone call. Prospecting we called it. Junk mail, as it later became known.

In sales school, they taught us to be able to handle this one objection more than anything else. I think it's as true today as it was then. Here's the objection.

"I don't know you, I don't know what you want. I don't know who you work for and I don't know why you're calling me. Oh, and I'm really busy."

Based on the content of emails I receive daily, it seems this lesson is not taught today. That plus many other lessons on integrity, work ethic, professionalism, sales process, and customer service have served me well in my post-IBM career.

Marketing Mentors: Jay Abraham

I became interested and hooked on Marketing as a career when I attended a 3-day boot camp hosted by Jay Abraham. "There are three ways and three ways only to grow your business." I can hear these words as if they were told to me yesterday.

But it wasn't yesterday; it was over 15 years ago by the best marketing mind I've ever met — Jay Abraham. (If you don't know Jay, you should look him up at www.Abraham.com)

Anyway, his three ways strategy stuck with me ever since and I make sure that I apply this principle to any company where I'm responsible for the marketing.

These three strategies apply to email marketing, but it applies just as easily to ALL marketing channels.

Three ways to grow your business with email marketing

One. Acquire new customers. Take stock of your email marketing campaigns. How many are designed solely to acquire new customers? Are you using autoresponders effectively to support your sales team to win new clients? Make sure your client acquisition campaigns are laser focused.

Two. Increase your average order size. At an email conference a few years back, I saw the perfect implementation of this email strategy by Sprint. In the transaction email that confirmed a new customer purchase, they added a few select accessory offers. What do you know? Their sales increased. You probably know this. "Do you want fries with your order?"

Three. Increase the reorder rate. This is a natural for email marketing and it's easier said than done. You must take some time to create a series of emails that provide chances for your new customers to place further orders.

If you use email marketing and apply these three strategies your revenues will increase.

And if you do them well, your revenue will increase exponentially. (I challenge you to pick a marketing channel or strategy that doesn't fit into one of these three boxes.)

Marketing Mentors: David Ogilvy

Ogilvy on Advertising and *Confessions of an Advertising Man* are two must-read marketing books by David Ogilvy. He became a master marketer by applying his skills at copywriting and testing to the emerging print and television mediums.

What he learned on the job, after investing millions and millions in ad testing we don't have to re-learn, we only need to heed his advice.

Read his books where he advises we learn how to write Headlines and Measure our marketing ROI. (More on these two topics specifically in the chapters on Email Copywriting and Split Testing. I'd say run away from ANYONE who claims to be a professional marketer but doesn't know Ogilvy's work.)

Marketing Mentors: John Caples

I have a copy of John Caples book, *Tested Advertising Methods* constantly on my desk. It's dog-eared and coffee-stained from constant use. There is a chapter in this book, which gives you 35 different styles of Headlines, which have proven to work and compared against Headlines which did not work. (Sound familiar?)

You'll be able to learn this method for creating Subject Lines for your emails, which beg to be opened. I've devoted an entire long chapter to this process later in the book.

9

THE IMPACT OF THE INTERNET MARKETING CENTER AND COREY RUDL

In 2005 I wanted to learn everything I could about Internet Marketing, so I went to the industry leader and asked to work for Corey Rudl at The Internet Marketing Center. Corey is the author of *The Insider Secrets to Marketing Your Business on the Internet*.

It was then THE source and process on how to get started selling and marketing online. Corey, in fact, hired Jay Abraham to help build their business model and much of their success can be attributed to his marketing methods. (Along with some pretty darn good copy.)

The three things the Internet Marketing Center excelled at were writing compelling copy, email marketing, and affiliate marketing.

I was like a sponge soaking up every tactic and technique they developed. As an Internet Marketing Mentor, I personally coached 72 businesses on Corey's methods. And, later, as their own VP Marketing, I was able to apply these principles to grow Corey's business.

The key result of working with these talented marketers is that I developed a love of email marketing. It required planning, creative work, design, copywriting, process, data management, statistics AND you could tell immediately if a campaign worked or didn't work.

When I wanted to create a marketing agency of my own, I knew it would be centered on email marketing.

ZinMarketing and the 3,400 email campaigns

Fast forward to 2007. ZinMarketing is conceived and formed with the sole goal of providing ROI-driven email marketing services for small business. I took the experience I learned of running email marketing campaigns with my 72 clients and as the VP Marketing at The Internet Marketing Center, and translated those experiences into a series of email principles that I used to set up and get ZinMarketing going.

In other words, I formed and launched this business going straight into the largest recession in my lifetime! Not only did we survive, but also we thrived and email marketing played a role in our own success.

We run hundreds of email campaigns each year. We have learned to be proficient at different software platforms like AWeber, Constant Contact, Campaigner, iContact, StreamSend, Infusionsoft, MailChimp, Lyris, MyEmma, ExactTarget, VerticalResponse, SendPepper, and others.

We learned how email campaigns work in over 104 different industries. We also followed and compared notes with other email and marketing experts to continue to keep on top of the ever-changing field of digital marketing.

I also authored and taught Email Marketing education courses for Social Media Marketing University and The Centre for Arts and Technology.

I tell you all of this because you should know what I'm teaching you in this book comes from firsthand experience and the school of hard knocks.

Not everything we did was a home run, but we did learn from each campaign and that experience has helped me to become skilled at ROI-driven email marketing.

HERE'S WHAT YOU'LL LEARN IN THIS BOOK

Overall, this book has three main goals.

1. To give you a FOUNDATION of the essentials of basic and advanced email marketing skills with the aim of improving your email marketing campaigns.

2. To get you started FAST, so you can improve your email marketing right NOW.

3. To keep you focused on what works based on proven tests and marketing techniques, which are based on experience and not fads or trends, so you don't waste your time.

The first thing you should do is read the FAST 5 and immediately try these 5 tactics. So far, these 5 have never failed to produce results!

THE FAST 5

For each of the FAST 5 you'll read the concept, its history and why it works, step-by-step how to execute the tip, and a checklist to remind you to follow the steps.

Fast 5 №1: Send a follow-up message in +7 days.

Pretend it's 1975 and you get an envelope in the mail. Quaint. You set it aside with your other mail and at some point, you sit down and see what you have. Bill, Bill, Letter. And, an offer from the Columbia House Record Club to join the club.

Right at that moment, you don't do anything with it. *But you don't throw it out either...*

Is that the end of it? What's happening at the marketing department at Columbia House?

Let's say that they get a response rate they measure to be 5%. Everyone is happy.

Yet someone in an advertising department somewhere, says: "Perhaps there can be more."

They try a test. They mail the same offer in the same letter again within 1 week. No changes.

Back to your household. You check your mail and another offer arrives. This time, you give it a bit more attention. You have had a week to mull it over, to think about it. You might even think it was your idea to join the Columbia House Record Club by then.

This time, you fill in the form, attach the stickers... and you become a conversion.

This is where human nature works in your favor. As Jay Abraham (who you read about earlier) would say: "Human nature is immutable."

People are not all the same, but **some** will do the same thing every time. In this case, people will make a decision, if you give them time... **and a reminder**.

Over time, this concept became a proven principle of direct mail marketing. Here it is.

Any time you send a direct mail piece, resend it 7 days later and you can expect conversions 20% to 40% of the first send.

Any time you send an *email* offer, resend it 7 days later and you can expect conversions 20% to 40% of the first send.

There are four variations of this strategy that we've tested.

1. Resend the same email to the same recipients with the same subject line.

2. Resend the same email to only the recipients who did not open the first time with the same subject line

3. Resend the same email to only the recipients who did not click on the offer the first time.

4. Resend the same email to only the recipients who did not open the first time with an updated subject line.

Because human nature is a bit predictable I know what some of you are thinking.

1. It won't work for me.

2. This isn't direct mail. Those days are done.

3. I don't want to annoy people by sending too many emails... they will be frustrated with me... all I will do is piss people off.

The simple truth is, this tactic has been around for decades, has worked in direct mail, and has been tested and works in email marketing. You can do the simple version of it or the more advanced versions and you will see results the FIRST time you try this.

Here's how to know people on your list don't hate you.

Send the follow-up message. After 24 hours check your inbox. You'll see no change in the number of nasty replies there.

Then check your sending report in your ESP. Check the unsubscribe rate and compare it to the unsubscribe rate from your previous message.

Generally, you can expect those numbers to be the same. That means your extra email didn't anger people enough to unsubscribe. At least not any more than ANY email you send.

Now, check your results. Did you get 20 to 40% of the results of your first mailing? You're welcome :-)

Fast 5 №2: Separate news and offer in your newsletter

Okay, I'm not sure where I learned this one from, but it has NEVER failed to work, and in a few cases it has worked GANGBUSTERS.

Here's the setup. (Read on if you send a newsletter each month, and if you include something for sale in your newsletter also.)

Imagine the typical newsletter. It has a fancy design. It has articles to read. It has some advertising in the right-hand column.

It's probably being sent out each month to everyone on the email list and the hopes are that the advertising will help sell a company's products or services.

There is an entire chapter coming up about how to do a newsletter so we're not going to worry about that now. We're only going to make ONE change to this newsletter... and here it is...

Separate the 'news' and the ads and send them in different emails. That's the only change you have to make.

Here's what happens and why this works.

In the traditional newsletter you are taking design thinking from the old days of sending a printed newsletter, which is based on the model of a newspaper. There are columns, headlines, and ads. The problem is this layout DOES NOT WORK VIA EMAIL. (Remember we'll come to this later.)

People don't go to email to look for and read your exciting newsletter from top to bottom, left to right. They go to email to decide if they should delete your message, read it now, or come back later. Attention is short, and at a premium. For your message to work, it has to be easy to digest and act on. Mixing news and ads makes that **more** difficult, not less.

Let me tell you a story.

At one point I had 2–3 writers producing a marketing newsletter that we sent out via email every week. It was long, often more than 20 pages.

The content was FANTASTIC! At the end of each newsletter, we had a section reserved for our weekly marketing offer. The strategy was, give good information and readers will still be there 20 pages later where your marketing offer is waiting for them.

There was only one problem. The content was so good, and the newsletter was so long, it created a new behavior. You can smile if this is you. It certainly is like me.

You know it's long, and you don't have time to read it now (after all, you were clearing out your inbox at last check), so you create a special 'NEWSLETTER' folder and either copy or put a rule in place to move the newsletter to the folder... *only to never return.*

Your newsletters don't get read, and your marketing offer (usually time-sensitive) doesn't get clicked on.

Here's what to do differently.

Leave your newsletter editorial and news the way it is. No need to touch it at this stage.

Take your marketing offer out of the newsletter (that's correct, NO marketing offer in the newsletter) and create a **second email**, which only has ONE marketing offer in it.

Here's what now happens.

You readers read your newsletter and feel favorable towards you because you *gave* them something of value. (See the upcoming chapter on reciprocity and why it works.)

They **appreciate** you because of it.

Then 3 to 5 days later, send your marketing offer in a single short separate email.

Basic level skill is to simply separate the two. Don't touch either one. I have seen some amazing results doing this.

Advanced skills would be to have a newsletter done properly (see Chapter 7) and then to write killer copy for your marketing offer (see Chapter 4) and your results will be even better.

Fast 5 №3: Remove anyone who has not clicked in 12 months

If you have been mailing people on your list for months and months and years and years, you may have fallen into a routine. Perhaps even are in a rut.

I had a client that we sent a weekly offer to every Wednesday, week after week, year after year. New people were being added to the list daily. After 5 years, there were people who had been on the list that long, or longer. Longer, because when we created the list some older customers were added. Each week we would have decent open rates and respectable click rates.

You probably know that if your readers fall into three categories. People who open and read many of your emails. People who have clicked on only one of your emails. And people who have *never clicked on anything you've sent them.*

One metric that should matter to you is your open rates. And your open rate should be an **accurate** reflection of what's happening when you send your message.

Let's say that every year 1,000 people never open anything you send them. Each year your list of dead weight grows and grows to be a larger % of your list… and as a result it looks like your open rate is declining (all other things being equal) so you start taking more and more drastic measures to bolster your open rate, when in fact, there is nothing you can do to affect those unresponsive names.

There is also a risk of keeping an old, unresponsive email address on your list. After a period of time, some webmail service providers (think free services like Yahoo mail) will reclaim an unused or abandoned email address and turn it into a Spam Trap. Then they monitor that email address to see who continues to send emails to a dead address. They know it's dead because they control it.

Continuing to send emails to a **Spam Trap** can affect your sending reputation and that can impact if your email message goes direct to the recipient's inbox… or to the spam folder.

The longer you let this go, the bigger the risk to your sending reputation.

Here's what you do.

Create a segment of all people who have not opened ANYTHING you have sent in the past 12 months. This is a really important statistic to know. It could be that only 20% of people on your list have not opened a message. It could be 80% of people on your list have not opened a message.

We'll talk about this in a later chapter but what would you rather have?

A list of 100,000 people (80% who are dead) or 20,000 people who you can get good data about open rates and behavior?

Human nature makes you want the large list (almost everyone thinks bigger is better) and it's more impressive to tell your friends, but the 20,000 people who are active in the past year are better for two main reasons:

1. Your risk of spam traps in the list is much reduced.

2. Your open rates will more accurately reflect what's really happening.

I know your objection. I've heard it before. "Mitch, what if there is ONE guy on there from 2008 that will open something or even buy something? I can't risk losing them." Mmmmm. Will you risk losing your entire ability to send or even risk having your messages start to show up in the spam folder? It's not worth it.

If someone hasn't opened ONE of 162 messages (just guessing) that you have sent, they aren't interested in you. Period. End stop.

[ADVANCED STRATEGY] If you want to make sure you don't miss any real people off your list, there is one thing you can do.

Send an email to everyone on your "haven't opened in the past 12 months list" and say something like this:

> SUBJECT LINE: We hate to see you go
>
> Perhaps we haven't sent you information that suits you or perhaps your interests have changed but we'd like to ensure you want to continue to hear from us.
>
> Click here to stay on our list and continue to get <insert benefit here>.
>
> Best Regards,

At least that way you can sleep at night knowing you didn't remove anyone by accident.

Fast 5 №4: 80/20 segment your list

One of the common email practices I see with prospective clients and clients is the notion of having 'an email list.' And, literally, they have just that.

They have ONE list that includes all emails ever encountered by their company.

They send them a newsletter.

Or they hammer them mercilessly with email offer after email offer.

Or they ignore them all together because they haven't got their email marketing processes built yet.

Do you know the Pareto Principle? Also known as the 80/20 rule? You can read more about it on Wikipedia, but basically it means that 80% of your output comes from 20% of your input.

You might say 80% of your revenue comes from 20% of your customers. Once you're aware of this concept you'll see it works in many, many situations.

Let's look at how it might apply to your email lists. Let's say you have one list, which includes, new prospects, old prospects, customers, blue-chip customers, and past customers... basically everyone.

If you were having an inventory clearance sale do you think that each of these segments will respond to your offer equally? No, not really.

If you had to guess, 80% of your opens might come from your customers. Maybe 80% of your inventory clearance sales might come from only 20% of your names.

The single biggest thing you can do to help your success is to find a way to identify your 20%, the 20% that can do you the most good.

This can be tricky.

Let's start with some basics. Let's say you have a good old-fashioned inventory sales campaign in mind. You plan to offer 20% additional off while supplies last.

The old way.

Send an email to your full list with the offer: 20% additional off while supplies last.

A better way.

Separate your full list into customers and non-customers and send two different offers.

1. 20% additional off for our best customers (You're seeing this before the general public because supplies are limited, and we want you to have first opportunity.)

2. 20% additional off for new customers. (You're seeing this because we would like you to try our products and thought 20% off might get your interest.)

Suddenly you get to use language that shows a better relationship. It's more personal and, as a result, it's more effective.

The 80/20 Way

Separate your full list into customers who have been the most active in the past 3 months and send them an email, which tells them they get 20% additional off on their next purchase and they get a head start on everyone else because they are a preferred VIP.

Send them a second message (see Fast 5 tip #1) telling them you are about to release this offer to others but wanted to make sure they had a chance to use the 20% offer.

You see the shift in thinking?

We've gone from an offer-centric campaign (20% for all) to an 80/20-centric campaign. An offer based on your past spending habits will perform better.

Campaign thinking plus the ability to create matching copy will generate a much better overall result.

Fast 5 №5: ONE offer per message

This one is a real challenge to teach because the emotional barriers to trying it are high and it's very hard to continue to follow this strategy.

Here's what most people think to themselves. "I'd like to send an email to my list [they are probably thinking their ENTIRE list] and let them know about our upcoming <insert the upcoming thing here>. While I'm at it, I should let them know about <offer #2>."

It seems simple and makes sense because your LOGICAL marketing brain is telling you, "readers will read both offers and make up their mind which is of interest to them."

By now you should know, *logic has nothing to do with marketing.*

It's all emotion and irrational behavior and unpredictability and human nature.

By placing two offers in one email you are making it harder, not easier for your reader to decide what to get excited about. Probably the best way to show this is to simply give you a made-up example.

Here's the old way. (don't think about the copy, we'll be doing copy improvements in a later chapter)

> Subject Line: SALE pricing on our top 5 bestsellers
>
> We appreciate you being a preferred customer so for 5 days only you can get 10% off our top 5 bestsellers.
>
> Use coupon code TOP5 at checkout. <u>Visit our website</u> to get your 10% off.
>
> And don't forget we'll be holding a gala event this Friday evening where you can see the new fall line and win some cool prizes.
>
> <u>Visit our website</u> to register for the gala.
>
> Best regards,
>
> Small business.

The proper strategy is to send TWO emails, one for each offer. It would then look like this.

> Subject Line: SALE pricing on our top 5 bestsellers
>
> We appreciate you being a preferred customer so for 5 days only you can get 10% off our top 5 bestsellers.
>
> Use coupon code TOP5 at checkout.
>
> <u>Visit our website</u> to get your 10% off. Best regards,
>
> Small business.
>
> P.S. You only have 5 days to use this coupon<u>. Get 10% off now.</u>

This is the copy for email #2.

> Subject Line: Attend our gala this Friday evening
>
> You're invited to our gala event this Friday evening where you can see the new fall line and win some cool prizes.
>
> <u>Visit our website</u> to register for the gala. Best regards,
>
> Small business.
>
> P.S. You have to RSVP in order to be eligible to win prizes. <u>RSVP here</u>.

Every email campaign you write will tempt you to toss in the interesting (to you) things that are coming up *just in case someone is interested.*

But if you're interested in the BEST results, separate your emails into one offer per email. Combine this with FAST 5 tip number 1 and you are suddenly doing email the way the professionals do.

CHAPTER 1

HOW TO ACQUIRE EMAIL ADDRESSES, BUILD YOUR LIST, AND GENERATE NEW LEADS OR CONTACTS

Learning how to collect more email addresses is a great skill to have. If you don't do this at all, one year from now you will not know anyone you can send an email to. If you do this half-heartedly one year from now you might have 1,000 people you can send an email to.

If you use all the techniques in this chapter, you might have 10,000 people you can send an email to.

Which one do you prefer?

It's a horrible feeling to say, "I wish I had started this sooner." Let's begin.

FIND YOUR AVATAR

An avatar is just another way of saying, 'target market' or 'ideal client' or 'audience'. Whatever you call it, doing this exercise is a critical marketing practice that most companies never do or haven't done recently.

The point of knowing your avatar in email marketing is twofold:

1. By knowing who your best avatar is, you'll be able to craft relevant and compelling offers because you know whom you're talking to.

2. When you write email copy, you'll be able to keep your avatar in mind and they will feel like you're talking to them and them alone. Very powerful stuff.

Here's one way to find your avatar. Simply follow these steps.

1. Run a report of your best customers or ideal prospects and look for common elements. It can be anything.

2. Try to find some common demographic. Think about gender, geography, average order size, age, or any one of a million other characteristics.

3. Try to find some common behaviors. They comment on your social media pages, they call customer service, or they use your rewards program.

4. Get personal. Do they have a dog, a BMW, a golf membership, a fancy job title, kids, or college degree?

5. Put a name to the face. Give them a name and identity. One of the best copywriters I know will go so far as to think "which of my friends" fits this description best. That becomes the visual for their avatar as they write.

Here's an example. A flower shop says:

"My ideal customer is Mary. She is married and 55 years old. She lives within an hour's drive of my location and orders flowers for her own customers each week. She runs a small business and drives a BMW. No kids but 3 dogs and is very active in her local community."

Think of this avatar every time you sit down to write an email. You'll find your offers become more relevant and your copy gets more personal. You'll see why this is even more important when you read the chapter on segmenting your list and writing powerful email copy.

Start by thinking of your avatar BEFORE you start creating your campaigns to collect email addresses.

DESIGN A WINNING 'ETHICAL BRIBE'

You'll remember Jay Abraham from the earlier marketing mentor section of the book. I first heard Jay use the term 'ethical bribe' when describing how to generate leads.

You absolutely have to think of WHY someone would give you his or her email address before you think of the WAY in which you would collect an email address. This is one step that is often overlooked when talking about how to build your list.

A great ethical bribe poorly presented will probably work better than a weak ethical bribe properly presented everywhere!

Here are a few ideas of ethical bribes to get you started:

1. A free report
2. A whitepaper
3. A case study
4. Free chapters in a book
5. A new customer offer
6. A new customer savings coupon
7. A free subscription to your newsletter
8. A free trial of your product, service, software...
9. A shipping-only offer on first sale
10. A product sample
11. A free assessment
12. A free analysis

This should spark some ideas for you to create your own ethical bribe. Try to make it as compelling and powerful as possible. Advanced marketers will create several offers and do testing to find which offer pulls the highest conversions.

Here's an example of one of our offers where we trade a 30-day training course for your email address:

zinmarketing.leadpages.co/30daystoemailmarketingmastery/

Spend time thinking about this and *do not skip this step!*

WHERE TO PLACE YOUR ETHICAL BRIBE ON YOUR WEBSITE

This section is really short, and the instructions are easy to follow. Yet, for some reason, you can look at 95 out of 100 websites on the web and see people do not do this. Put yourself in the top 5% right away.

Here's where you place your opt-in form (offering your ethical bribe) on your website.

On Your Homepage Above the Fold

If your website has 2 or 3 columns, simply place your offer in the top-right or top-left spot. If your banner is so large it doesn't allow for placement like this… make a smaller banner and allow room for your form.

Add a Sign-Up Option in Your Navigation Bar

This one is also simple to execute and again, you'll probably only find 5% of websites you visit have this. However, on many e-commerce sites you'll see that a link to **Log In** is often located very close to a link to **Sign Up**. This is the concept you want to follow. Add a link called Sign Up on your left navigation stack.

Put Your Own Banner Ads All Over Your Website

Create a simple banner ad and put it all over your site. Place on the right column, add to your footer, and place it in every blog post. Suddenly you'll find that more people will make it to your list.

Now you have placed a method for people to get your ethical bribe by giving them a chance on your website, no matter where they enter your site or what page they travel to.

USE A SQUEEZE PAGE

You'll need a squeeze page to execute two of the top three pages

You may have heard the term *squeeze page*, or you might know it as a landing page. No matter what you call it, we're referring to a page, which has only one purpose, to fulfill your ethical bribe offer.

Here's an example of a landing page from a company that sells you landing pages:

https://lp.leadpages.net/4step-landingpage-f/

You should notice right away that the top of the page is dedicated to making the offer with the headline "Free LeadPages Tutorial Shows How We Created Our Highest Performing Landing Page." That's a pretty good offer and your action is likely to click the big green button "Free Instant Access."

In order to create a landing page for your business:

1. Create a separate page on your website with a name like www. yoursite.com/lp-offer1. I like to use the initials LP in the name so you can sort them by name if you develop lots of different landing pages. Make sure you also name them so you can recognize the offer and version when you see a long list later on.

2. Use a large easy-to-read headline on the top of the page so your reader can see your offer right away. Keep images and other distractions away so the headline is easy to read.

3. Put your opt-in form right on this page above the fold.

4. Generally you won't have other navigation on this page, which can distract your visitors and take them away from the offer. A best practice is to make your case as to why someone should give up his or her email address. Even if you have a killer offer, it always pays to remind people why they should take it.

That's really the big difference between a landing page and other pages on your website. How many landing pages do you have on your website right now?

> BONUS TIP: Do you have a custom 404 page on your site? A 404 page is the page that displays when your visitor types in a page that does not exist.
>
> Most 404 pages say, "Oops, you found a page that does not exist." The copy then tries to move you to a page on the site that might help you with what you're looking for.
>
> Instead, place your ethical bribe offer in place of the text, which says, "Page does not exist."
>
> You'll be surprised how many people will sign up to your offer when it's presented.

USE A POP-UP

You all know those annoying pop-ups. You're on a site minding your own business and suddenly a window is blocking your view!

Just so we're all on the same page. It doesn't matter that you like or dislike email pop-ups, what matters is that if you use them properly, your sign-up rate for new subscribers will soar.

Here are three examples of email pop-ups that are well executed and warrant a closer look.

Pop-Up on the Side

Let's take a closer look at this example. You can tell the site is Blinds. com and they are interested in scooping up your email address. This pop-up option is less intrusive. It doesn't jump out at you and just sits quietly to the side and makes a clear offer to trade your email address in exchange for a chance to win.

It's a good execution of an email offer that goes above and beyond just a form on the page.

Pop-up with ethical bribe

Here's an example of a pop-up which is targeted specifically to buyers. A 10% coupon is the ethical bribe to get a visitor to sign up. This is a good example of a simple offer.

The headline says it all. For these types of pop-ups make sure the offer is simple and easy to explain.

Of course, the more compelling your offer, the better.

Pop-up with mandatory enrollment

This is an interesting pop-up. In order to actually get to the site, you MUST give up your email address. When you click on the **why?** link, it explains that as a member-driven site they have to know who you are in order to let you participate in their offers.

It's a solid 'reason why' that makes sense. That's an important aspect of a 'reason why'... it has to make sense. If you don't believe it, they likely won't either.

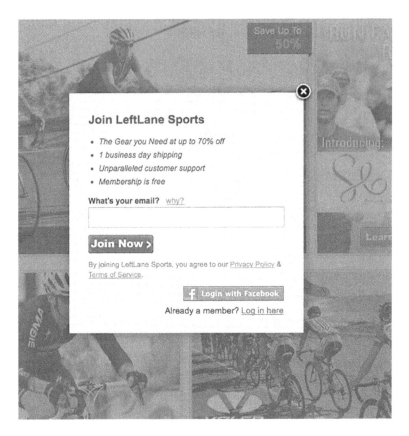

Think again about using email pop-ups on your site. They really don't do any harm to your brand and they can increase your conversion of visitor to subscriber dramatically.

ADVERTISE AND PROMOTE YOUR ETHICAL BRIBE EVERYWHERE

And I mean everywhere.

So far we have focused on increasing your lead flow and opt-in rate by working on conversion concepts on or near your website, but you should be considering where else you can make your offer.

We were working with an e-commerce provider and we calculated that every email address that joined their list would earn them $24 in profit (not sales but profit) every year. That means they could comfortably spend $2 dollars for each email address gained (assume they were able to target their avatar) and earn their investment back *fast!*

Knowing that every $2 spent you could earn $24 within the year, how much would your budget be to gain new email addresses?

If you discovered you could only earn $1 in margin for each $2 you spent, you would approach this differently. In some businesses, it is worth it to lose money on your customer's first order so you can profit from ongoing sales. Think about this for your business.

Knowing your numbers means you can:

1. Collect emails on the tradeshow floor

2. Collect an email at the end of every sales call

3. Run Google PPC ads

4. Run Bing PPC ads

5. Do FACEBOOK (This is an entire course by itself, but you can do this free or in their paid advertising accounts and target your avatar with pinpoint accuracy)

6. Advertise Twitter

7. Run paid Pinterest ads

8. Run paid LinkedIn ads

9. Buy ads in compatible newsletters

These are just a few examples of places you can advertise your ethical bribe to get new contacts. There are hundreds of other sites that have paid advertising. Don't limit your thinking here.

If you want more leads and subscribers, look for more places to make your offer.

SHOULD YOU USE A SINGLE OR DOUBLE OPT-IN?

If you're not familiar with the term Opt-In, it simply means the process of someone joining your list by filling out a form. Chances are you have filled in lots of forms from newsletters to contact us requests.

What you might not have discovered is the running battle between fans of the Single Opt-In and the fans of Double Opt-In. For starters, there is no one way that is best. There are pros and cons of each. Make up your own mind on this.

Here's what's involved.

A single opt-in means you fill in a form, click on the 'Submit' button and that's it. You're on the list.

The pros are: easy for subscriber, fast, with no additional steps.

The cons are: an incorrect email address can end on the list, malicious emails can be added to the list, there is no relationship built with the reader, and your sending reputation can suffer because of your lower list quality.

Some systems will allow you to add a Captcha field at the bottom so bots can't attack your list. This helps somewhat with your list quality.

A double opt-in means you fill in a form, click on the 'Submit' button and the subscriber receives an email which says 'Please confirm your email address'. When they click on that link, they are added to the list. That confirmation email is the double part.

The pros are: you can build a better connection with the subscriber, a subscriber has to really want to be on the list to do the extra step so the quality of subscriber is better, and no bad or improper email addresses end up on your list.

The cons are: you will have a smaller list since about 40% of attempted opt-ins will not take the step of confirming their email address.

It's as simple as that.

1. Larger, lower quality list with a single opt-in process.
2. Smaller, higher quality list with a double opt-in process.

Make up your own mind on this. I know super successful marketers that will ONLY work with single opt-in processes and I know super successful email software providers who will ONLY work with double opt-in processes. Either is just fine.

Just decide which is your pick and run with it.

YOUR OPT-IN PROCESS IS YOUR FIRST CHANCE TO MAKE A GOOD FIRST IMPRESSION

Imagine this. A person, who is your exact, ideal client, is online and discovers your website. Yay. A new visitor. Then they read your website and with interest fill in a form to download a free report.

What are the steps they go through before they start to read the report?

Usually, it goes like this: (this is a double opt-in process below)

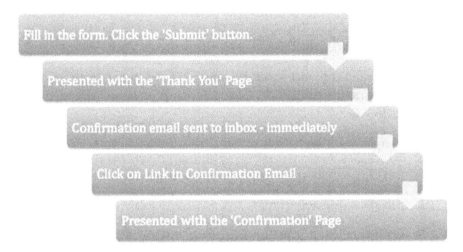

Fill in the form. Click the 'Submit' button.

Presented with the 'Thank You' Page

Confirmation email sent to inbox - immediately

Click on Link in Confirmation Email

Presented with the 'Confirmation' Page

(Read the Case Study #1 in this book to see an example of this in action)

This seems pretty straightforward but there are lots of ways to get this wrong. Here's how to get it right.

Once someone has clicked your 'Submit' button, the first question on their mind is: "Did this work properly?" "Will I get the thing I was promised in the form?"

That's your first step. Make sure you have some form of copy on the "Thank You" page that tells the reader their action worked. Now that worry is free from their mind, ask yourself this question: "What is the most important piece of information I can place on the *Thank You* page?"

If you look at these pages, you'll see 99% (no kidding) there is nothing special there. No offer. No information. No note from the CEO. No secondary form to ask more info. This is a big missed opportunity. SPEND THE TIME TO THINK HARD ABOUT THIS AND PUT A SECONDARY OFFER ON YOUR THANK-YOU PAGE.

While your visitor is reading this page, the confirmation email is sent to their inbox. Again, most confirmation emails have plain copy that basically says "Please click on this link to confirm your email address."

The most important thing you can do here is to explain WHY you want them to confirm. Remember: up to 40% of people who filled in the form originally don't click on the link to confirm their email address.

By telling them why, you'll increase the number of people who will join your list.

You could even try this. Give them an incentive to click the link. You can deliver on the incentive when they click and are taken to the Confirmation page.

The point of this whole discussion is that this opt-in process is your first chance to make a first impression. Most companies just set up the technical steps to make this work and in the rush to get things done, don't think about making a good first impression OR taking the opportunity to use your Thank You and Confirmation pages to their best advantage.

COLLECT MORE EMAIL ADDRESSES WITH SMART MOBILE OPT-IN DESIGN

If you don't read the Motley Fool financial website you're missing out. Not that I'm a financial wizard or anything but they exemplify good content writing which is used to drive a big list.

Here's what I mean:

The creation of great content that people read, combined with an opportunity to get more information by joining a list is a common practice for online marketers.

What's not common is bloggers and companies doing it well.

I'll walk you through the Motley Fool process on a mobile phone so you can see the process and their mobile opt-in design (which is fantastic!).

I'm reading a Motley Fool article. Here is a screen cap from my phone.

●●●●○ AT&T 📶   11:19 AM   📞 56% 🔋

fool.com

investor to consider.

One of the dirty secrets that few finance professionals will openly admit is the fact that dividend stocks as a group handily outperform their non-dividend paying brethren. The reasons for this are too numerous to list here, but you can rest assured that it's true. However, knowing this is only half the battle. The other half is identifying which dividend stocks in particular are the best. With this in mind, our top analysts put together a free list of nine high-yielding stocks that should be in every income investor's portfolio. To learn the identity of these stocks instantly and for free, all you have to do is click here now.

R.I.P. Internet -- 1969-2014

At only 45 years old... the Internet will be laid to rest in 2014. And Silicon Valley is thrilled. Because they know... *The Economist* believes the death of the Internet "will be transformative."

In fact, the CEO of Cisco Systems -- one of the largest tech companies on the planet -- says somebody's going to bank "14.4 trillion in profit from

↪ Share   ⌄

You don't have to read the article to see what I see. Just make a note that the content is easy to read, and you'll see a link to a free list of nine high-yielding stocks in the copy. That link is followed by a call-to-action that is pretty compelling.

"To learn the identity of these stocks, instantly and for free, all you have to do is click here now."

I know some of you have clicked on these pseudo-links (that's how good they are) but I don't want you to get distracted.

Here's where they take you. (Keep in mind I'm on my phone)

●●●●○ AT&T 🔋   11:20 AM   📞 56% 🔋
fool.com

The Motley Fool.
To Educate, Amuse & Enrich˙

Free Report!

Secure Your Future With 9 Rock-Solid Dividend Stocks

To get the names of the 9 top dividend-paying companies selected by Motley Fool analysts, simply enter your email address in the box below.

I've often told you about the difference between the copy I see most often... "Free Newsletter" and this offer. This one has a headline, a logo, the benefit, and a clear call-to-action. Look at the design.

Is it fancy? No.

Is it hard to read? No.

It's perfectly designed for mobile.

And what do they ask you to do? Fill in the least amount of information possible. See.

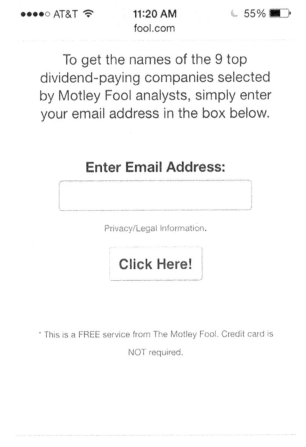

●●●●○ AT&T 📶   11:20 AM   📞 55% 🔋▶
                    fool.com

To get the names of the 9 top dividend-paying companies selected by Motley Fool analysts, simply enter your email address in the box below.

Enter Email Address:

Privacy/Legal Information.

Click Here!

* This is a FREE service from The Motley Fool. Credit card is NOT required.

Essentially you are looking a great mobile opt-in design in action. They even use a button other than the "Submit" button. You couldn't find a better example if you tried.

Keep this in mind when you're planning your mobile offers. You have to make these changes to maximize your return on email marketing. More people are getting in on the game and it's getting harder to stand out.

RUN THIS DAILY REPORT: OPT-INS VS UNSUBS

This is one of those small things that professionals do and amateurs rarely do.

With email marketing, there should be one question on your mind every day, "Is my list growing or shrinking?"

Here are two ways to monitor this process.

1. Check at the same time each day and make a note of your list size. Growing is good. Shrinking is bad. You'll see this right away.

2. You'll get more info if you compare new people joining your list (opt-ins) vs people who unsubscribe (unsubs) from your list.

Either way, make sure you track these numbers. It's an early warning system that will tell you if something changes and you need to take corrective action.

CHAPTER 2

HOW TO REACH THE INBOX AND NOT BE ACCUSED OF BEING A SPAMMER

One of the most common questions or fears people have about running email campaigns is the fear you'll be accused of being a nasty spammer.

You worry about all kinds of bad things happening you have no control over. You worry about your reputation. You worry about your account being shut down. And you have other fears you can't even articulate.

This next section will give you a good foundation of how to protect your reputation, keep your email account, and not have trouble with your campaigns.

USE AN ESP

The first step to not being accused of being a spammer is to not spam. Sorry, couldn't help myself.

ESP stands for Email Service Provider and is one way for you to start earning your sending reputation.

Generally speaking, you'll discover three main ways to send email in higher volume. For some people sending email in batches of 50 or 100 names in their Gmail account is how they evolved into running email communications.

If you're doing this now, just stop it. It's labor intensive and doesn't give you many of the advantages of an ESP. (more on this later)

You may know some of these ESPs by name. MailChimp, Aweber, iContact, Constant Contact, MyEmma, Campaigner, Get Response are just a few. There are literally hundreds of them.

Spoiler Alert

It doesn't really matter which one you choose. All of them are capable of sending email campaigns in high volume and have features to help you.

However, they are not all the same. In a market with hundreds of ESPs, each is trying hard to differentiate themselves with unique, interesting, or useful features.

You will find people who absolutely LOVE one of the ESPs noted above. You'll also find an equal number of people who absolutely HATE one of the ESPs above. At any given moment you'll find someone wanting to switch from one to another because of some real or imagined infraction.

The reality is that there are features you don't know you need until you've been around the block a few times. You'll also find you can go for years on a single platform and run amazingly powerful campaigns.

A word of caution. Once you have your ESP, work with them as much as possible because switching can be way more trouble than it's worth and once you've switched, you'll discover something that you took for granted in one ESP is missing in another.

Spend more time and energy focused on creating GREAT email campaigns and less time worried about why your ESP doesn't do what YOU want it to do.

Also, all modern ESPs have support departments and no matter which one you pick, you'll be using their support at some point. These people can help you A LOT so don't be afraid to reach out.

By using an ESP you will start building a sending reputation. If you follow good practices, you'll have a good sending reputation, which will help you reach the inbox.

FOLLOW CAN-SPAM, CASL, AND THE NEW EU LAWS

There are rules. More than rules. There are laws. You'll want to make sure you are on the right side of the laws. They're quite simple really. You can't change them, and you should NOT ignore them.

CAN-SPAM was introduced in 2003 in the U.S. Since I'm not a lawyer and shouldn't be giving legal advice, your best bet to understand CAN-SPAM is to visit en.wikipedia.org, search for 'CAN-SPAM' to ensure you are compliant.

The good news is that by using an ESP to send your emails, their policies ensure you follow the rules.

In 2014 Canada followed suit with legislation of its own. Search Wikipedia for 'Bill C-28' and you'll find their law. The rules are different and if you are based in Canada you'll want to make sure you stay within the law.

The single biggest piece of the CASL law is that there is no implied opt-in. Every email address has to explicitly state they want to be on your list. With that in mind, you will want to consider leaning towards a double opt-in if you operate out of Canada.

TEST BEFORE SEND

Here's the interesting catch-22 about spam filters. The rules are not published anywhere. On top of that, there isn't one set of rules. If the rules were published then spammers would simply have to read them, and then be able to circumvent them. Plus, the rules change constantly.

You've probably heard advice, "Don't use the word FREE in your subject line. Spam filters are sure to grab your message." It's really a whole lot more complicated than that.

Some spam filters are 100% content based. These filters will grab your message if it looks to contain typical spam content. It's a constant battle.

Other spam filters are 100% reputation based. If you have a history of sending non-spam looking messages, your message will hit the inbox.

Some spam filters are a combination of the two. 75% content and 25% reputation. Or 40% content and 60% reputation.

Today, many spam filters are behavior based. A sudden spike in spam complaint levels and suddenly you may find your future messages get sidelined in the spam folder.

Because there isn't really a way to know the rules and they change constantly, here's what we do.

Create a TEST LIST and include all your seed email addresses in the domains you want to make sure allow your messages through. That means your test list will include addresses from @gmail.com, @yahoo.com, @hotmail.com, @comcast.net, @aol.com, @msn.com, @me.com, etc.

Then send your message to this list. Don't use the test system or server. Send it exactly the way you would send it to your target list. Then check your inboxes and see if your message is in spam or not. Although there are different types of software that will simulate this feature, their guess is as good as yours whether a message will get caught up.

You'll be surprised by your findings. Sometimes, every message is okay except you'll see it in a Yahoo spam filter. Or Gmail will catch it. Sometimes you'll be blocked in almost all of them.

If you have the time, you can tinker with your copy and see if that changes things. As an example, on one mailing we found that using the word FREE 3 times was okay, but 4 times did get our message blocked.

If you haven't seen it already, most ESP software has a feature which will rate your message on a scale based on how likely it is to be caught by spam filters. For the type of messages most of you will be sending, you'll be unlikely to be ranked too high but it's good to know where you stand.

THE ROLE OF THE UNSUBSCRIBE REPORT

You'll find that every time you send a message you will get someone who unsubscribes. Over time, your unsubscribe rate will settle in a narrow range. Please don't take this personally. You don't know why people unsubscribe, and trying to guess will drive you crazy.

Unsubscribes are best compared as a percentage of opens. Seeing 100 unsubscribes can be unsettling until you remember you sent out 200,000 emails.

Studies have shown that the most common reason people unsubscribe from any list is: emails aren't relevant, interests have changed, or too many emails were sent.

By keeping an eye on your unsubscribe percentage rate, you'll be able to tell when it spikes or slowly starts to increase. That should be a message to you, your audience is reacting to your content or something has changed in your list makeup.

HOW OFTEN SHOULD YOU SEND EMAILS?

How often to send an email is a pretty common question.

Mostly, you're worried that you'll send too many messages and people will think poorly of you, your brand, and your company.

Think about your favorite subject or hobby. If you're into something, it's unlikely you'll be saying, "I sure hope I don't see anything more about that today."

Usually the issue isn't frequency, but relevancy. Your messages are more about you. Or you're off topic.

I assure you if you're sending information and emails that tap into something your audience is crazy about, they will transfer that affection to you.

Sometimes this is hard to explain.

It goes like this. They do not care about your company BBQ or your new logo. They care greatly about themselves and have their radar on high watching for things that are good for THEM or make them feel a certain way.

Now, the answer to the question about frequency. It doesn't matter. Some companies and people can successfully send an email every single day. Others, every week. One thing is for certain: *you can send emails more often than you think.*

We often tell clients is to double their current frequency. Watch your unsubscribe rate. If it doesn't spike or start to rise, you can keep going at that rate. Try it.

CHAPTER 3

HOW TO SEGMENT YOUR LIST

Many people seem to be curious how their email marketing stacks up against others. Seems legit. Especially if you wonder how your competitors are doing. First, let me say this. You are best served by comparing yourself to your own past achievements.

Having said that. One thing that very few email marketers do is segment their list. Many, many companies have ONE list. Everyone is on it. Everyone gets the same email newsletter.

That's not optimizing your use of email, so you're probably leaving money on the table. Possibly lots. What happens when you segment is you are able to speak directly to people in specific terms and not general terms. Once you see some examples of how to segment, you'll immediately know how to segment your lists.

Here are some ideas to get you started.

BUYERS AND NON-BUYERS

Trick question. What is your process to move people from your prospect list to your customer list? If you only have one newsletter list, you don't have a process. Everyone just goes on your mailing list and you send him or her a newsletter and call it a day. (And possibly wonder why it costs so much for your ESP account)

Let's assume you had not one, but two lists. A customer list and a prospect list. If you were interested in growing your revenues, you wouldn't send them a newsletter with faux news in it, you might send an offer to your customers to motivate them to buy more from you.

You might also send a different offer to your prospects to convince them to take that first step and become a customer. (At which point you would send them an offer to motivate them to buy more from you!) See how that works?

The point is, there are two different thinking processes going on here. One is nice. The other grows your business.

BUYERS INTO 80/20

Now let's take this a step further. You probably already know that not all of your customers are created equal. Some buy your product, or take your service. They pay on time. They are grateful for what you do for them.

Others. Well. They don't seem happy. Ever. They grind you down on your prices and have high, even impossible expectations.

Try this exercise. Separate your customers into two groups. One group, you can call your blue-chip group. They generate the most revenue. They are the easiest to deal with. They were even easy to sell.

> One of my best marketing mentors told me to try this with your blue-chip customers.
>
> Call them up. Day or night. On their cell. In a chat message.
>
> Say this script. "Hi. I've been thinking about you and wanted to check in and see how things are going with you. I have a question. What is your top

challenge right now with <insert your product/service offering here>"

After they tell you. Respond with. "Interesting. Let me brainstorm solving this problem for a few hours and I'll get back to you with an idea or two."

Then create an offer, which solves the problem.

Although this isn't precisely an email campaign, you could just as easily follow this process with a survey email. Take the responses and deliver a new product offering.

If you simply did this one exercise, how would your business grow?

Why wouldn't you do this with ALL the names on your list? The answer is simple. You don't really want more of the customers which want to pay less and get more while being unhappy the whole time.

SEGMENT BASED ON BEHAVIOR

What's one of the easiest behaviors to measure in email marketing? It might be seeing who opened a past email and who did not.

Let's say you have been sending newsletters out this year. Would you think you have two different audiences?

After six months of the year, you will have people on your list that *have never opened even 1 email*. You think it's not possible but it's quite common. The real question you should ask is, "Is that 10% of the people whom I've sent an email to, or is it 50%" I've seen both, and it will tell you something about the relationship you have with your readers.

Once you have your list separated into people who have opened your message or messages and those who have not opened a message you can decide what to do with it.

For example. If you send out a message and you have a 20% open rate, you can now send two different follow-up messages.

The message you send to your opens might be more of a reminder message or a case study or benefits message to encourage more interest from your reader. They might have been interested the first time, just busy when your message arrived.

The message you send to the people who did not open your message can be completely different. Different subject line. Different offer. Different layout. Don't worry about annoying people. They didn't see your first message!

A different type of behavior you might think about is to segment people based on them clicking on a specific link. Make your follow-up message more relevant.

All ESP software I've ever seen has the ability for you to create a list of people who opened a message or who clicked on a link. Don't be shy to use this information in a follow-up message.

What would you say to someone who had opened your last 3 messages but had not taken action?

What would you say to someone who had NOT opened your last 3 messages?

SEGMENT BASED ON PRODUCTS PURCHASED

One of the most powerful marketing strategies is to make follow-up offers to people who have already made a purchase from you.

Here are some ideas to get you thinking about this. You have control over several factors.

One is timing. Let's say you set up an email string, which follows a new customer's first order. You can make a secondary offer 1 day later. You can make a secondary offer 1 week later (to allow time for the first order to be delivered) and then you can set a series of automatic messages over time.

What you'll be testing here is which combination of products or offers produce the best results.

SEGMENT BASED ON THE SALES FUNNEL

You probably have a sales funnel. Even if you don't have it documented yet. Generally, you'll have categories, like lead, prospect, qualified, proposal sent, closed. Some funnels have many steps to them, and others like this one have only 4 or 5.

The way you would use email here is to create a message series designed to move people from one step in the process to the next.

What would you say to move someone brand new from a lead status to a prospect status?

What information would help move them along? What call to action would tell you they were making the move?

The secret to this style of segmenting is to think about the steps and *movement*. It's movement that gets people from stranger to friend to customer, as Seth Godin would say.

SEGMENT INTO ACTIVE AND INACTIVE

If you have sales reps, or an order desk, this simple email campaign will give you an immediate boost in leads and sales… immediate.

One of the fun aspects of my business is I get to experiment with new email strategies that I read about or hear from others. It's a bit of an adventure because I never know for sure how they will perform.

Generally, I'll test these campaigns on my own list and leads to see what happens.

Here's an example of a simple email campaign that I ran earlier in the year… with amazing results.

My open rate was 28% higher than normal and my inbox was filled with responses within 24 hours of sending this email.

Its simplicity will make you scratch your head, but it works!

Simply create a short email with the subject line: "Are you still interested?" and send them this email. DO NOT add more copy to it. Of course you can replace 'email marketing' with your service but otherwise, *don't mess with the language.*

If there is any test that can demonstrate to you if your subscribers actually read your messages this is it.

If you need a shot in the arm to bring some of your old leads back to the table, this is it.

You'll be surprised at the power of this simple concept... just ask.

Hi steve,

Are you still interested in email marketing?

Either let me know your best number or give me a call at the number below.

To a Great Year!

Mitch

Mitch
ZinMarketing.com
T: 707 320-2507

CHAPTER 4

HOW TO WRITE POWERFUL EMAIL COPY – EMAIL COPYWRITER'S CHECKLIST

I think learning how to write compelling copy is one of the best marketing skills you can learn. Not all words are created equal. Some words will trigger certain emotions in your reader and move them in the direction you want.

It's tricky, though, to look at words and decide if they are compelling or not. Learning how to write copy is simply a skill like any other and you can learn it too. Like I mentioned earlier, one of the first things you can do is get a copy of Tested Advertising Methods by John Caples. There are many great writing lessons in there.

Follow these specific guidelines and you'll be on your way to creating emails that get the click.

ADVANCED AVATAR EXERCISE

Earlier I had you do an exercise to try and get a clear picture of your target audience.

Here's what we came up with:

> A flower shop says: "My ideal customer is Mary. She is married and 55 years old. She lives within an hour's drive of my location and orders flowers for her own customers each week. She runs a small business and drives a BMW. No kids but 3 dogs and is very active in her local community."

Before you sit down to write your email, take this exercise one step further. Get a picture and post it somewhere where you can see it. Next, take your message, your offer, your story, and explain it to them... out loud. Listen to how you sound. What words are you using?

Now lean into it. Try to *convince* them about the merits of your argument. Mean it.

Is it easy to understand? Are you clear?

Now you can write it like you'd say it. Like you're talking to this person. You'll find it easier to feel like you're in their shoes. Like you know them. Like what you're saying matters.

This is an extra step that the professionals do. And it shows.

FIND AND USE YOUR 'VOICE'

It's time to create an email. You sit down, think about what you want to say... and then you start to write...

... like a stodgy university professor. (Unless you are a stodgy university professor, then you're okay.)

The challenge is. Reading email is not usually your primary task. It's the thing you have to do in order to get on to real work. You try to do it fast. You try to delete things that don't help you. And when you do find something you want to read, you don't want to be put to sleep with dead, boring copy.

It was explained to me like this. "Try to write it the way you would say it and it's important your listener gets it."

Writing with a voice means giving your email some color, character, or personality. It's not easy to do because for some reason our entire school days are devoted to formal writing with perfect grammar.

If you're funny, be funny. If you're a rocket scientist, use it. If you're German, use it. If you're from the hood... you know.

People always have and always will want to deal with other people. Especially ones they can relate to. It's where trust begins.

FROM + SUBJECT LINE + FIRST SENTENCE COMBO

1. Use a Shorter Subject Line

There have been enough studies of subject line length that this one should be an easy best practice. Although you'd be surprised at the number of times I see long subject lines from big companies or top marketers.

Anything less than 45 characters or so is good. Anything longer than 55 characters is not so good.

If you can nail it in less than 12 characters you might just catch a wave.

The famous "Hey!" subject line from the Obama 2012 re-election campaign comes to mind.

During that campaign, the email team (20 or so people) tested every variation and combination of subject lines and messages they could imagine and the "Hey!" version generated the highest open rate AND the highest donation rate.

Just strip it down to the shortest message you can. People are busy.

2. Match the Subject Line and the First Sentence

This is tricky but well worth it! Take the concept from your subject line and extend it or clarify it or make it more compelling in your first sentence.

This has two purposes.

First, if your reader is using a preview pane to screen emails with, they will have more information to motivate them to read the balance of the message.

This is a good reason to NOT use the popular "If you can't read this message" text many ESPs insert for you. THAT doesn't make me want to read it at all AND it tips me off to expect a marketing message.

Second, if your subject line and the first sentence don't match up in theme or concept, you're running the risk of breaking the tenuous thought that's in their head as they make that fleeting decision to read the rest of the message.

Stay on topic.

3. Match the Subject Line with Your FROM Address

Who is the email FROM? Do they know you? Are you a stranger? Is your FROM address a company name or the popular info@?

If you can make the FROM address personal then you can also use a personal subject line. If your email address is corporate you may have to be a bit more formal in the subject line.

FROM addresses are a big reason why people open an email... don't forget about it.

4. Write Your Subject Line Like a Marketing Headline

This topic alone is worth writing a small book or report about. Simply put. If you want to get someone's attention you have to think like a world-class copywriter.

And that means headlines.

So learn how to write good headlines. Can't go into it here because it's just too big a topic. But let me say this.

If you're getting tired of the heat and someone sends you an email that says, "Escape the sweltering heat" you're going to look at it.

You're about to buy a new truck and you get an email that says "Save

$4,000 off your next truck purchase" you're going to look at it. Can't sleep? "Learn 3 sleep secrets of world travelers"

If your headline is tuned in to your audience you're going to get killer open rates. If you can connect your subject line to your reader's interests and problems you're going to get great results.

You won't do as well with clever, tricky, ambiguous, or funny subject lines.

Try it. You'll see.

MAKE YOUR SIGNATURE LINE CHOICES

There are only two best practices here.

1. Use the same signature line you would on your normal correspondence. If it's simple. Keep it simple. If it's formal. Keep it formal.

2. Make sure your signature line is from a person. Don't try to use 'The Team' or some other general sign off. People want to hear from a person, not a committee.

Try not to over think this. The goal is to make an email, which looks like it was sent from a real person and sent individually. You're also trying to make your bulk emails looks as much like your personal emails as possible. Fancy formatting and a different signature line won't do that.

36 SUBJECT LINE IDEAS AND STRATEGIES

Good subject lines draw you into the message where the message does its job of sending you to the landing page.

With that in mind, your subject should be able to catch your reader's attention and pair with the first sentence to draw the reader in.

(That's the reason you don't want any of those 'fine print' messages at the top of your email. Many ESPs force you to put one there by default. Get rid of it.)

These subject line ideas are drawn directly from John Caples book, Tested Advertising Methods, on how to write good headlines. The concepts work equally well in email subject lines.

1) Use the word "Introducing"

   Introducing new pricing for our special clients

2) Use the word "Announcing"

   Announcing the best cycling jersey on the planet

3) Make your subject line sound like an announcement

   Just released. Our newest table saw.

4) Use the word "New"

   New way of reaching hard-to-find prospects

5) Use the word "Now"

   Now you too can write copy like a pro

6) Use the word "At Last"

   At last, low pricing for the rest of us

7) Put a date into your subject line

   One day only. Friday, May 4th.

8) Write your subject like a news story

   Man bites dog. And saves 15% on his auto insurance.

9) Feature your price offer IN the subject line

   Top quality cycling bibs – $139

10) Show your discount

    Leather wallet only $19.95 (regular $39.99)

11) Write your subject line like an end cap at the store

    Buy One Get One pricing today only

12) Lead with a payment plan

    Order today in three easy payments

13) Make a Free Offer

    Free 14-day trial (Don't worry, the word *Free* by itself is not enough to get you blocked.)

14) Offer valuable information

    Insider's guide to email marketing

15) Tell a story

How I paid off $25K of debt in 10 months

16) Use the words "How to"

How to get the raise you deserve

17) Use just the word "How"

How you can get our member-only price today only

18) Start with the word "Why"

Why powerful subject lines touch your readers

19) Begin with the word "Which"

Which method will stop your snoring?

20) Begin your subject line with "Who else?"

Who else wants to earn money in their sleep?

21) Use the word "Wanted"

Wanted. 10 people to beta test our new software

22) Use the word "This"

This is the best performing dishwasher anywhere

23) Use the word "Because"

Because your plants keep dying

24) Start with the word "If"

If you think your car is old, you'll be amazed at this story

25) Start with the word "Advice"

Advice to people who are late on their payments

26) Use a testimonial in your subject line

    As seen on Oprah

27) Offer a test

    Can you tell the difference between Coke and Pepsi?

28) Use a one-word headline

    Hey

    Shy?

    Worried?

29) Try a two-word headline

    Try now

    Dog fleas

    Blue chip

30) Try a 3-word headline

    Save money faster

    Get fit overnight

    Find true love

31) Warn your reader to delay their purchase

    Don't buy home insurance till you read this

32) Speak directly to your audience

    I'll show you my email marketing secrets

33) Call out your audience

    To small business owners strapped for time

34) Ask a question

   Did you know you can skip the line?

35) List a benefit with a statistic

   Saves 23% on your gas mileage

36) Use the word "Get"

   Get the love you want

Try these tips when you sit down to write your email.

Our best practice when we write copy is to write 10–12 versions of a subject line BEFORE we craft the email copy. Often, you'll see one version that will jump out as more interesting and powerful than the others.

Good luck.

HOW TO WRITE KILLER EMAIL MARKETING COPY

Sometimes what you *don't* put in your copy is as important as what you do put it.

When you write or review your email copy your **single most important consideration is clarity**.

Clarity trumps most everything else when you're writing. Is your message clear? Is it easy to understand? Are there any extra topics or sentences that take away from your key message?

When you re-read your message, are there extra words or sentences that take away or confuse your main message?

You'd be surprised how easy it is to slip in an extra thought that can sidetrack your reader. What you're trying to do is move your reader along a path to your call to action.

Once those extra words are in there, you can start to become attached to them and have a hard time getting them out of the way. Be cool, calm, and collected... then delete them!

WRITE ONLY TO ONE PERSON

Sometimes when you're writing, you forget your avatar and use language, which speaks to a general audience.

You want to avoid saying "Thousands of people like you want to get a new job" and try something direct like "You want a new job?"

Anything you say which shows your reader they are the only one you are speaking with works best.

FEATURES AND BENEFITS ARE NOT THE SAME

If you've ever been through sales training, you'll be familiar with the concept of features and benefits. It is a surprisingly simple concept, incredibly powerful... **and no one uses it**. I'm not kidding. Once you've had this lesson, go read ANY sales or marketing document and 9 out of 10 of them will have no benefits.

People are looking always looking to discover what's in it for them. That's where the benefits come in. Your emails become waaaay more effective if you are able to connect the dots for them.

One way to think of the difference between features and benefits is to think of it this way. Features are what something is or does, and a benefit is what it does for you.

Here's an example:

Our car has a diesel engine. (what it is)

Vs

Our car has a diesel engine, so you'll get better gas mileage, and that saves you money. (what it does for you)

[Insert any feature here] + [add any benefit here].

One more thing. If you feel like you don't have the benefit quite right just say your sentence and ask the question. SO WHAT? You don't have to yell it, but you'd be surprised how this will focus your writing.

Our car has a diesel engine. [So What?]

So you get better gas mileage. [So What?]

And that saves you money.

You could drag it on, but that's a way more compelling sentence.

One way to use features and benefits is with bullet points. Write out all the features that are important to your audience. Don't worry about the benefits yet. AFTER you have the features listed then go back and add in the benefits.

Do the same with your email body copy. Go back and re-read the copy and look for room to add a benefit statement to the end of your statements. [So What?] <insert your benefit here>

"YOU" VERSUS "I" ORIENTATION

When you sit down to write your emails, odds are pretty good you're going to start with something like…

"I'm sending this email to inform you…"

"I'd like you to know about…"

"I'm the CEO of…"

"We're a software company that..."

These are all examples of an 'I Orientation.' Here's the thing. People don't care about you. They don't know you and they have other things on their mind. You have to reach them by talking to them directly.

A marketer once told me you have to reach them via the radio station that's playing in their head constantly. W.I.I.F.M. That stands for **What's In It For Me**.

Remember. "Human nature is immutable." People are always thinking, evaluating, wondering. "What's in it for me." It's just the way it is.

That means you have to start your sentences and email with language that sounds like this.

"You can..."

"You will..."

"Get..."

"Learn how..."

"How to..."

It's a small but powerful difference yet you will receive emails every single day, which ignore this fundamental marketing principle.

The best way to put this into practice is to write your email in draft form. Focus on your message. Then go back and look for orientation. Are there more 'I's than 'you's? Simply rewrite the sentences to match. Once you make the copy changes, you'll find there is a difference how your email feels.

And it will be way more effective too!

USE A CALL TO ACTION AND 1 MESSAGE PER EMAIL

This is a big one!

It's big because everyone, EVERYONE, thinks they can put whatever they want in their email and people will read it and logically decide which of the 7 things you let them know about they will read and then click on.

Here's what really happens.

- Your email is confusing. They delete it.
- Your email looks long. They delete it.
- Your email is boring. They delete it.
- Your email's formatting is messed up. They delete it.
- Your email font is too small to see on a smartphone. They delete it.
- You talk down to them. They delete it.
- Your message isn't relevant. They delete it.
- They don't know how it would apply to them. They delete it.
- The phone rings or Facebook messenger pings. They forget you... and delete it.

You need to send a relevant, compelling, benefit-laden, interesting, easy-to-read email that they can't ignore and won't delete in the first 7 seconds.

So here's the plan.

Before you sit down to write your email, think of ONE Call To Action (CTA) you want from your reader. Here's an example. I'm sending a Black Friday email offering a 50% off coupon. My goal is to send them to a specific product page that I think they would be interested in so they can use their coupon.

Now you can write your message.

By having only one concept, message, and CTA in your message you make it easy for your reader to deal with your interruption.

You will ignore this advice because you will take a logical approach. You will argue that people can read about your Black Friday offer AND your Open House in one message. Don't fool yourself.

Send two messages. Make your *crazy* Black Friday offer and then send a *personal* invite to your Open House.

Someone, somewhere, said. "Telling is not selling!" If not, I said it here.

GENERAL VERSUS SPECIFIC

Let's assume that when you send emails you would like people to believe what you write. You're certainly not sending emails so that the reader can say "Liar, liar, pants on fire!".

That's exactly what they think when you use general language like:

> Thousands of happy clients
>
> All this... and more
>
> Most of our customers find
>
> Better gas mileage
>
> Huge selection

You will be more believable if you use language like this:

> 3,459 happy clients
>
> 7 main benefits
>
> 80% of our customers find

9% better gas mileage

1,882 items in stock

It's understandable. You're trying to show yourself in a more favorable light. Or look larger than life. Like a puffer fish. What happens is that you look like you're making something up.

Use specific language and facts and you will have more credibility. A note for all you brand people. All the branding in the world won't help you if your copy doesn't show credibility.

THE PROPER EMAIL LENGTH

During one stint in my marketing career, I had a marketing department that was responsible for sending 8 to 10 different emails each day for different campaigns.

We were sticklers for split testing and we tested everything possible to find optimal email marketing strategies.

One thing we discussed, a lot, was, "What is the proper email length?"

If you know about direct-response copywriting, you know there is a debate that has been raging for years (and years). The debate is, how long should your direct-response sales copy be?

Some argue that copy should be as long as it takes to explain your offer and address all the potential objections before you get to the call to action.

Others argue that if copy is long, the reader will get bored and leave before you get to the call to action.

The debate rages on and has carried over to email.

In our company, and with our audience, we proved again and again that short copy works over long copy in the email. The shorter messages got the best response whether we measured just email statistics or whether we measured conversion data also.

Having said that. I have seen some very credible case studies, which demonstrate better results from long copy. More than one have shown this.

What it boils down to is this. Great long copy beats poor short copy. Great short copy beats poor long copy.

The only way to know for sure is to TEST for yourself.

EMAIL COPYWRITER'S CHECKLIST

1. **Subject Lines.** Write out 8–12 different subject lines for your email and split test them if you can. Use variations of the 36 types suggested.

2. **First two lines.** Make the first two lines in your email match your subject line and entice the reader to keep reading. How does it look in a preview pane when you test it?

3. **The email must be relevant.** Double-check that you have a relevant message for your audience and their expectations. Don't go too far astray.

4. **Personalization.** Sure, you can use first name in the subject line and copy, but try to find other data you can personalize your message with. Super powerful.

5. **Write it like you would say it.** Don't try to use big words or sound important. Use casual language and make it sound like you mean it.

6. **Write for Grade 6 level.** Studies have shown that the simpler your message is, the more effective it is. Go for clarity above anything else.

7. **Paragraph length – 3 lines only!** Keep it short. Keep your paragraphs short. It should look easy to read.

8. **Develop a voice.** Take advantage of your unique style and voice. You vs I test. After you write your draft, go back and read to see if you are talking about yourself too much. **W.I.I.F.M.**

9. **Use benefits.** Benefits and bullet points and email are very effective. Use them.

10. **Use bold, italics.** Don't be afraid to make your text stand out. Don't be AFRAID to make *your text stand out!*

11. **Short better than long.** Reread your copy to see if you have extra words or sentences that just take up space but don't make the message stronger.

12. **Clear call to action.** What do you want your reader to do? Tell them. Show them. Direct them.

CHAPTER 5

USE HUMAN NATURE IN YOUR FAVOR
Based on *Psychology of Influence* by Cialdini

THE PSYCHOLOGY OF INFLUENCE AND EFFECTIVE EMAIL MARKETING

One of my favorite marketing books is ***Influence: The Psychology of Persuasion*** by Dr. Robert Cialdini. I first read it a few years back and have since re-read it twice. Its message is that powerful... for marketers, that is.

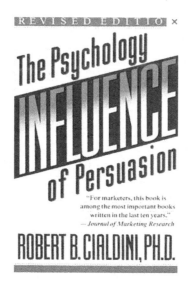

Dr. Cialdini outlines 6 methods of influence and explains why each method works. One of my favorite marketing experts is fond of saying human nature is immutable. It is and has always been the same.

Many would argue that today's modern society has changed human nature, but I agree that humans have and continue to have the same basic needs.

Which brings us to persuasion and email marketing.

RECIPROCITY

One of the elements of persuasion that is built into human DNA is how we respond to a good deed. Dr. Ciandini calls it *reciprocity,* and good marketers know how to use it to its fullest.

It goes like this…

Someone gives you something. You then have a primal, subconscious, powerful urge to return the favor. No, you don't feel it and you can't fight it. It's just there. Reciprocity.

A few simple examples of reciprocity at work:

- A sales rep buys his prospect lunch
- You are offered a sample in the aisle of your food store
- You sign up for a 'FREE' trial
- Your neighbor lends you a tool

Each of these events creates in you a need to do something in return. You feel obligated. It's just there.

How to Use Reciprocity in Your Email Campaigns

What is it that you can 'give' your email readers? The gambit can range from something simple, like a hint or tip, to something concrete like a free sample or trial account.

Generally speaking, if you think of the concept of reciprocity when you are designing your email campaigns, over time you'll create stronger and stronger desire on behalf of your readers to reciprocate.

It could come back to you in many, many ways.

Reciprocity works the best when you don't expect something in return. You just let it happen. Human nature is doing your marketing for you.

COMMITMENT AND CONSISTENCY

This section is short, but it is POWERFUL, so listen up. The top marketers understand human nature and work with it instead of fighting it.

Let's start with consistency. People, in their mind, strive to act consistently with their belief system. If they think they are cheap, they buy cheap. If they think they are luxury, they buy luxury. If they think they are unique, they buy unique.

In other words, people will buy based on who they think they are, not what you think about your offer. This is a hard concept to grasp when you're selling luxury goods, and you, yourself don't see yourself as a luxury buyer. You can't quite understand why someone would pay top dollar when you do price comparisons like a fiend.

The best way to use this concept in your email campaigns is simply to try and create campaigns and offers that best match your audience. If you're selling to coupon cutters, you will have a tough time with a full price offer. If you're selling to wealthy clients, price discounts aren't your best bet. Think about it when you're creating your campaigns.

Commitment is also a powerful side of human nature you can use in your email campaigns. It is similar to the concept of reciprocity. Here's how it works.

If you can get someone to make a small commitment to you, they become much more likely to agree to a bigger commitment later on. In terms of email sales, you might consider if you can find a small simple front-end offer, which you can follow with a larger more valuable offer later on.

In today's world of social media, this is the value of engagement. Early engagement in a product offer or launch becomes a marketing tactic to help you get a bigger commitment later on.

Try breaking your email campaign into two parts. One small offer or act your audience can do before you make your main offer.

SOCIAL PROOF

Social proof is all around us. Facebook has it dialed in.

"Monkeys see, monkey do" is a well-known expression for a reason. People will follow a crowd.

To prove this to yourself, just go stand on a busy street and look up at a tall building. It won't be long before others join you and you might just be able to draw a fairly large crowd... who are staring at nothing with you!

How can you use this in your email campaigns? Two ways.

1. In your copy include some evidence that others support your offer. You might say. 'Over 1.2 million sold' or '9 out of 10 Dentists use this product'

2. You could build a campaign based on testimonials. Include not 1 but 5 testimonials in your copy. Show that others are on board and your audience is likely to follow.

Simple. But powerful.

LIKING

People are more likely to buy from people they like. Period.

It's even more likely if they think they are similar to you. Your goal here is to make it easy for your audience to like you.

Who says you only have to send an email. What if you link to your Facebook page or Instagram account to demonstrate your likeability? Suddenly, you become a real person to them and not some faceless company trying to sell something. This is particularly important online.

Video gives you even more ability to be likable and show your similarity to your audience.

Use this concept in your email campaigns by linking to a video or Social Media accounts to make it easier for your audience to like you.

If they do, they are more likely to buy from you.

AUTHORITY

I ran an email campaign for a client a few years ago. I was creating the compelling case for why their audience would want their product. After doing almost all of the research, the client told me one thing. I immediately threw out my compelling case and replaced it with this tidbit. Can you guess what I wrote?

"As seen on Oprah"

That little sentence was more powerful than any copy I could write. That is the power of authority.

For your email campaign, what authority can you claim? Are you a supplier to a Hollywood Movie Star? Does Apple use your software? Does Warren Buffet take your investment advice? Do you have a quote in the Wall Street Journal? Did you write a book?

Don't forget to use all of these tools in your emails to make people believe you.

This one reason an email from the Founder or CEO is more compelling than an email from "The Team".

It takes some effort but it's worth it.

SCARCITY

Have you ever been to an auction? Have you ever placed a bid? How do you feel when someone outbids you? Does your heart race? Are you suddenly worried you won't get the item you're interested in?

A small company called eBay figured this out on a massive scale. We've all paid more than we would have liked because ONE item is getting away from us. Someone else will get the thing we want.

That's the power of scarcity.

It can be real in the case of actual limited supply. Unscrupulous marketers can also manufacture it in many ways. For example, when someone tells you an ebook is in limited supply, your emotional mind starts to make you worried you'll miss out, and your logical mind goes "hold on. An ebook is unlimited. It's not in limited supply."

If you're going to use scarcity in your email campaigns to trigger that emotional response, you have to do it honestly and in a believable way for it to work.

Here's an example:

This online webinar will sell out. (not so good)

We only booked 50 call-in lines for our online webinar and this invite is going to over 10,000 people. (pretty good)

You might have seen a countdown clock. That's another way of presenting scarcity.

You might have seen an inventory count which says "4 left on hand" which also uses scarcity.

Scarcity is a pretty powerful concept, so you should find a way to work it into your email campaigns and copy.

FINALLY

After reading these little snippets on human nature, you are saying smugly to yourself. "Well of course everyone wants to buy from someone they like."

However, did you sit down and look at your messaging in that context? Have you been able to find ways to change your landing pages, email copy, and offer to be more personable and likeable?

If you did, you are acting like a marketing professional. If not, you are acting like an amateur.

CHAPTER 6

HOW TO BUILD EMAIL PROCESSES AND AVOID MISTAKES

USE AN EDITORIAL CALENDAR

There's nothing magical about an editorial calendar. Put it on paper or set up a common Google Editorial Calendar or throw it on a whiteboard in someone's office. How you do it isn't really all that important.

You just need to do it.

Here's an example of how it works. Let's say you use email for the following purposes:

1. You send a monthly e-newsletter

2. You have two trade shows approaching in the next 90 days

3. You have an excess of inventory and want to make a special offer

4. You have a new product on the way

Take your editorial calendar and post these events in the dates they occur.

Then create your ideal email sequence for each one.

- You'll only send your e-newsletter once
- You want to send 2 messages 2 weeks in advance of your two tradeshows
- You want to send a 3-message sequence about your inventory
- You want to build some announcement excitement (pretend you're Apple) about your product before the announcement

Place these on the calendar and see where they fall.

HERE'S THE PAYOFF!

Once you see these emails on a calendar you can step back and see what this looks like **through the eyes of your reader!**

When you place the emails beside one another you'll suddenly see ways to make your message stronger.

HERE'S WHAT NOT TO DO...

Do NOT be tempted to take all the items and combine them into a single, comprehensive, efficient email. Do not do this!

Why?

Because it will sound like this. "Blah blah blah, tradeshow, blah blah blah sale price, blah blah blah new product." Your reader cannot be expected to stop everything and take the time to read this longer email and decide what's really important.

They can't and they won't.

QA PRE-SEND CHECKLIST AND PROCESS

We all talk about checklists and processes but the steps to create and send an email are the same every single time. Since one email is going to be seen by tens, hundreds, thousands, tens of thousands of people, a mistake can hurt.

The largest list I ever worked with was 7.2 million and I have to say sending to that list made me double and triple check everything.

Here's the process we follow, and we follow it the same way every time.

- Create your copy in a text editor. Run a spell check right there before you save the file.

- Create a test list in your email software and include as many of the following email addresses as you can: Yahoo, AOL, Hotmail, Gmail, Mac, Outlook, and any others you think your clients might be using.

- Send your message through the production side of your software to this full test list. (Many systems have a test message feature. We don't use that.)

- Read the email carefully. Look carefully at the following:

- The From address and From email is correct.

- The subject line is correct and is short enough to display in all systems.

- Read the message word for work and check for spelling, grammar, and word choice. (Go through it twice, once for accuracy and once for clarity.) (Did you see the typo in this paragraph? That's why we don't rely on spell check only.)

- Review your formatting on all the different systems. Did Yahoo drop your line breaks? Did your word wrap choices make the mobile device look odd? Are there strange characters suddenly?

- Read your email on a mobile phone. How does it look? Can you even read it? This is critical since as of 2016 probably 50% of your readership will check your message on their phone. If they

- can't read it, they aren't going to try very hard to see what you sent.

- Click on EVERY link and make sure it lands on the landing page you intend. If there are tracking codes, make sure they show up properly.

- Once you've clicked on the link, check that the landing page works. Sign up, purchase, test to make sure it works too. This is a killer if you miss it.

- If you are using personalization (like first name), make sure the data is inserted properly.

- Now read the message. Check facts like time and date and make sure they match what's on the landing page.

- Finally, take a deep breath and ask yourself, "Is this message clear, compelling, and does the call to action really work?"

Sometimes it makes sense to have someone else read your message because they might see something easily the author of the message missed.

No matter what edits you make to your message, even if it's a simple change, you'd be well advised to resend a full test.

If you don't go back through the test process, that's when a new formatting error sneaks in. It's pretty important to do this, especially when you're in a rush. Takes a few minutes but you'll save the headache of an embarrassing mistake.

HOW TO RECOVER FROM A BOTCHED EMAIL

This topic came up recently after I received an email with a broken link in it. Then I received the correction email.

In the next two days, I received two more emails with problems in them, so I thought I should give you a strategy or two on how to deal with fixing an email campaign with a mistake in it. Because someday, you will find yourself in this situation.

Before you do send, make sure you follow a pre-sending checklist and you'll reduce the chances of having a problem but...

It can happen to you.

How severe is your mistake?

If you have a typo, or bad grammar, or a format that goes wrong, don't worry about it. Most people realize you are human and will give you a hall pass. It doesn't help you to draw attention to it. Those that have seen it, and noticed, will have dealt with it and those that didn't see it don't need to have you point out your proofing flaws.

However, if you have a broken link, anyone who wants to click on it will be disappointed. You'll be disappointed too because you won't make any sales. A broken link means no sales for you.

Here's the fix for a broken link.

You have a few options. Here are a few that have proven to work well.

1. Resend the message exactly as is and add a comment in the subject line: [LINK FIXED] or [CORRECTION]. This style of fix is pretty straightforward and logical.

2. If you want to be more human about it, use a subject line like "Oops!" or "Our Mistake!" or "My Mistake!" Then add a short sentence to the beginning of the message and point out the error and the fix. This one is very human, and people *have to see what they missed*. It's human nature.

3. A simple apology and work well too. Subject line: We're so embarrassed! Then explain the problem and the fix.

In all of these situations, **make sure you are brief about it!**

Let's look at some examples.

[Link Fixed] Example 1

Take a look at the subject line and message below. The only change to the message is the addition of the [RESEND – LINK FIXED] text. The body copy remained the same.

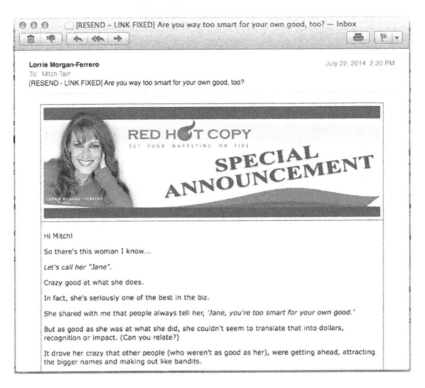

[CORRECTION] Example 2

In this example, the Oops text was in the subject line along with an explanation of what happened. I've seen this work particularly well if the subject line says only "Oops!" Humans are a curious lot.

Mari Smith
July 28, 2014 10:45 AM
To: Mitch Tarr
Oops - link fixed! NEW Facebook 101 training course

Uhoh! It seems our email system hit a technical glitch earlier today. My last email may have had weird strike-through text and dud links. Ugh! We've fixed the issue now so, in case you weren't able to properly view the message properly or access the Facebook 101 web page, I'm resending the email below. Thank you for your patience and understanding. I do hope to help you in the FB101 course if it's a fit for you! Warmly, Mari

Hi Mitch,

Due to popular demand, I just unveiled my newest online training course, **Facebook 101: Back To Basics!**

...and, since you are a valued member of my community, I wanted you to be among the first to know about it!

If you are a small business owner, entrepreneur, independent professional or marketing manager and you struggle to keep up with the constant changes on Facebook, and/or you want see measurable results on both your personal profile and business (fan) page... I'd LOVE to help you!

More Explanation – Example 3

This is another example of an Oops style message AND you'll notice I received this on my phone. That's why you want to be brief with your explanation. This message is particularly good because it's human. It has some personality.

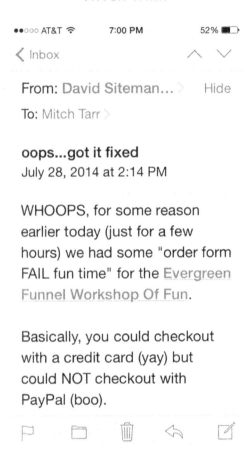

Keep these tips in mind in the event a broken link slips past you!

CHAPTER 7

HOW TO CREATE READABLE E-NEWSLETTERS (INCLUDES EMAIL NEWSLETTER CHECKLIST)

THE MYTH OF THE E-NEWSLETTER – WHAT YOU SEE IS WRONG!

Who here is old enough to remember how a printed newsletter used to look? They spent time on design. Like a newspaper or magazine.

I remember because my very first marketing department used to publish one. We sent it every month to our best customers. We tried hard to publish something interesting. The key word here is *publish*. Do you remember publishing software? Its sole purpose was to put the task of formatting print documents in the hands of non-professionals.

It's only natural that style of thinking was the way early newsletters were created. They were no longer newsletters... they were e-newsletters. Yet they had the same old design criteria as printed newsletters.

The only problem is they were sent via email. Some were even sent as attachments.

Fast forward to today (2018). You read your newsletter on a phone or an iPad or at your desk (it still happens). The formatting is just about the LAST thing that matters. What really matters is, "can I read the headline and the text easily and quickly?"

And it also matters that you have something to say.

This is my way of saying that in today's modern newsletter you can forget about ANY newsletter layout that's given to you by your ESP and your graphic designer. They are comfortable in the past.

You have to start by thinking about how to make your newsletter worthy of being read.

That means you have to let go of design thoughts and start to focus on content thoughts.

EFFECTIVE E-NEWSLETTER FORMAT

It wasn't easy to find a proper newsletter format but here is a pretty good example of a format that works. First I'll show you the image, and then I'll explain point by point which parts of this newsletter are done properly so you can get a proper design.

You don't need to read the copy in the newsletter. That's not the point.

1. SUBJECT LINE: If you're doing a legit newsletter, it's okay to simply say so in the subject line. You don't need to be tricky, clever, or hypey. (Is that even a word?) Simply state it's your newsletter. If your content is good. Trust me. People will be interested in reading it.

2. A SMALL banner is good to open the newsletter with. Keep in mind, not everyone will see it if they use preview panes in their email client so it could just as easily show up as an

empty space. Make sure you use good Alt text on your image.

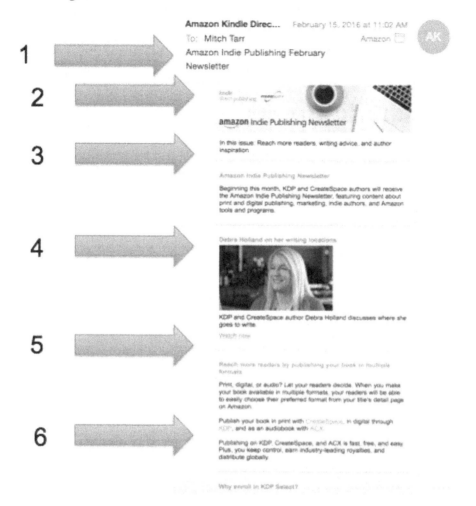

3. This is an excellent feature. It says "IN THIS ISSUE" and describes what's to follow. This little-used feature will pull people into your newsletter, especially if you hit on a topic they are interested in. Tell them what to expect and they'll keep reading. Ever watched a movie trailer? Same concept.

4. The orange text is a HEADLINE. Pioneered by print newspapers and effective for hundreds of years. I'd go with

it if I were you. Headlines tell the reader why they need to read the section. Skimmers will check headlines to see if you have something for them, without having to read the whole newsletter. Most people will delete an email without headlines… simply because it looks like too much work to read it.

5. Separating lines. I'll let you make up your own mind on these. Research has shown that ANYTHING that breaks a reader's path to keep on reading can be enough to also break their mental thread to keep on reading. If that happens and they stop. Well, you're done. Personally I think they are visually appealing, but, since they stop the reader from continuing their scan, I don't use them. Up to you.

6. Finally, the copy. Short paragraphs and simple links. Make it easy to read and pull them to your blog or YouTube channel or website to read more. That way you can track who clicks on what and learn more about your audience. *Reread this last sentence. It's important.*

Hopefully, you now have an idea of what an effective newsletter looks like. Next, I'll show you how different newsletter styles affect you.

3 WINNING E-NEWSLETTER STYLES

You have choices on how to set up your newsletter. Don't let the template designs dictate what those choices are.

I'll give you three options along with the pros and cons of each.

1. **Long Copy.** The first newsletter style is pretty straightforward. One column. Headlines. Relevant images. It should look a lot like the example above.

2. **Lead Story + Links.** Another way to make a newsletter simple and easy to read is to follow the directions above and change the content so you have a feature story.

Your feature story should be something that really helps your readers. After you have your main story you can follow with a series of useful, interesting, or helpful links.

Resist the temptation to pad the links with your product offers and services. Your readers will appreciate you much more if you provide value.

One advantage of this style is that you can look at your reports and discover which links, resources, and information are of most value to your readers.

3. **Story Leading to Blog Posts.** A lead-in looks something like this.

Watch Me Build a WordPress Website in Under 30 Minutes.

If technology is driving you crazy, this might be a perfect time to learn a new method to create a good-looking website. Usually, I'd show you a video with a voice over but to make it easy for you to get the site you want I've created a step-by-step guide. Read more here.

Write two more story leads like this and now you have a short powerful email newsletter which allows your reader to pick which of the three stories is most interesting to them.

Some will read all. Some will pick only one. Again, that info is important to help you better understand your audience.

PROPER LENGTH AND FREQUENCY OF NEWSLETTERS

I once had a marketing department that published an email newsletter on Friday of each week.

It was AWESOME, and it was literally 20-plus pages long. The content was fantastic.

Here's what happened.

People got our newsletter. They were busy. It was Friday. They wanted to read it but soon realized that reading a 20-page newsletter was a big challenge. So they found an answer.

They set an email rule that captured our email from their inbox and put it in a dedicated folder called 'Newsletters' so they could return and read it later.

Guess what?

They never did.

Don't create too much content or send it too often. If you get a rule written for your content, you have failed.

CHAPTER 8

WHAT REPORTS TO READ AND HOW TO INTERPRET THEM

Let's start by looking at the basic building blocks of email marketing. Here's what you need to track:

1. Open rate

2. Clickthrough rate

3. Bounce rate

4. Unsubscribe rate

OPEN RATE

FORMULA:

unique opens / sent emails = open rate

321/3999 = .0802 or 8%

What it means: *Open rate* measures how many people open the email you send. Keep in mind some of these measurements are more general indicators than precise metric.

Open rate is a relative number that you can only compare to *your own* other open rates. Trying to compare your open rate to open rates from other industries, other companies, or on other ESPs will only make you crazy.

If you have a weak or not relevant subject line last week and a powerful or super relevant subject line this week, you'll see a difference. Maybe a 20% compared to 30% open rate.

If you send a message to your best customers vs a message to your general newsletter list, you'll see a difference.

Just keep an eye on open rates so you'll know strong ones from weak ones. This gives you a feel for what appeals to your different audiences. Use that information to make content decisions going forward.

CLICKTHROUGH RATE

FORMULA:

unique clicks / unique opens = clickthrough rate

89/321 = .2772 or 27.7%

What it means: Clickthrough rates measure how many people who saw your message, clicked on a link in your message. It's a great indicator of how strong your offer is, how relevant your message is and how good your email copy is.

When you start seeing CTR (click-through rate) in the 30% range that means 1 in 3 people read your message and clicked a link. That's a great CTR.

Most ESPs will also tell you how many people click on each of your individual links. It's useful to check which of the links are most popular. Sometimes you want to discover which topics are of most interest and comparing clicks can tell you that. You'd be surprised at how often you'll be surprised it's not the one you expect.

BOUNCE RATE

FORMULA:

bounced emails / sent emails = bounce rate

155/3999 = .0387 or 3.8%

What it means: Email bounces can be a very long, very technical topic. What you need to know is that there are generally two types of bounces — a hard bounce or a soft bounce.

A soft bounce means your email didn't get delivered for some temporary reason. Things like the recipient's mailbox is full and can't receive more mail or the mail servers are unavailable and can't receive mail. Most ESPs will resend these messages automatically in the background for you so you don't have to worry about them.

A hard bounce is something like an invalid email address. A good example is when someone leaves a company and their admin deletes the email address. Your ESP will not attempt to resend this email address. Some ESPs will give you very detailed delivery information and others provide limited info.

The one thing you're watching for is if your bounces spike. It means something's potentially up with your delivery.

UNSUBSCRIBE RATE

FORMULA:

unsubscribed / sent emails = unsubscribe rate

17/3999 = .00425 or .4%

What it means: Your unsubscribe number is the one number which can quickly tell you if you've misjudged your audience and jumped the shark. Over time your unsubscribe rate will settle in a tight range.

As you change your email pattern and try different things, keep an eye on this number. If it starts to rise slowly, step back and think about your mailing patterns and content. What have you changed recently?

Watch for a spike in your unsubscribe rate. If it doubles or triples one day, your audience is sending you a silent message. Take heed!

Here's what this looks like in a spreadsheet.

Emails Sent	3999	
Open rate	321	8%
Clickthrough rate	89	27.7%
Bounce rate	155	3.8%
Unsubscribe rate	17	.4%

Use a tracking report

C	D	E	F	G	H	I	J
Mailed	Unsub	% Unsubs	Opens	% Opens	Clicks	% Clicks	Results
3097	6	0.19%	324	10.46%	64	19.75%	
2725	6	0.22%	246	9.03%	27	10.98%	
3080	11	0.36%	323	10.49%	6	1.86%	
3003	8	0.27%	316	10.52%	23	7.28%	
3019	11	0.36%	354	11.73%	0	0.00%	
2979	13	0.44%	303	10.17%	10	3.30%	
2981	11	0.37%	318	10.67%	56	17.61%	
1917	3	0.16%	121	6.31%	9	7.44%	
2938	6	0.20%	358	12.19%	60	16.76%	

Graph your data for better understanding.

What happened here?

ADVANCED TRACKING WITH GOOGLE

If you're using Google Analytics on your website, you will want to track your traffic sourced from email. If you don't know how to add Google UTM extensions on your links, visit this page and learn how:

https://support.google.com/analytics/answer/1033867

By using the Google URL builder, you'll be able to track all the traffic to your website and landing page and then using Google analytics you can watch the behavior of this traffic and how it converts. That way you can compare it to your other traffic sources.

FACEBOOK TRACKING PIXELS

In recent years the Facebook advertising platform has been getting stronger and stronger. At the time of this writing, one of the most powerful features is the ability to use tracking pixels to remarket to a website visitor.

Here's how it would work.

Let's say you have a segment of your list that has version 1 of a product and you want them to upgrade.

1. Segment your list in your email system.

2. Export your list from your ESP and upload it to your Facebook Ad Account. Set them as a custom audience. Facebook won't find all of your email contacts, but it might find 50%.

3. Make sure you have your Facebook tracking pixel installed on your site.

4. Create and send your email campaign

5. Create a matching Facebook ad campaign

What happens now it people who are on your list receive your emails in the series. At the same time, they would start to see a MATCHING Facebook sponsored post in their news feed, reminding them to take your offer. On top of that, if someone has visited your website from this campaign, you can create a DIFFERENT ad that acknowledges they visited the site and encourages them to return (perhaps with an extra incentive).

This type of integrated campaign is super powerful yet can be a bit tricky to keep clear in your head which audience segment is which.

KEEP AN EYE ON YOUR SPAM COMPLAINTS

Spam complaints happen. Even if you have a double opt-in list. Sometimes people forget they joined your list and sometimes they will click on the "THIS IS SPAM" button just to make a point.

If you are getting close to or more than 1 spam complaint per 1,000 emails sent, something is not right and needs your attention. If you're above this level, you will likely get a call from the deliverability team at your ESP.

CHAPTER 9

ADVANCED SKILLS

HOW TESTING WILL IMPROVE YOUR RESULTS (SPLIT TESTING CHECKLIST)

Create a Tracking Spreadsheet

A/B Split tests – Two Main Styles

There are a group of professional marketers out there that believe strongly that tracking and measuring the ROI on your marketing money is one of the best ways to optimize your spend. They also believe that testing your marketing campaigns is one way to gain the highest possible return.

I'm one of those types of marketing professionals — and we apply that philosophy to email marketing where the tools and statistics are readily available to help you test your way to a better ROI.

Yet few people run A/B split tests regularly. Sometimes they don't know how (I'll tell you how in a second) or sometimes they don't know what to test (I'll give you ten things to test in a second). There are two ways to run split tests.

First. You can split your list into two groups. If your software allows a split test, they will give you a random split of A/B. If not, you'll have to create a custom field named "Split" and populate it with an 'A' value and a 'B' value.

Now you'll have an 'A' segment and a 'B' segment. Simply send one version to the 'A' segment and your alternate version to the 'B' segment.

Compare the results and voila, you're split testing. Over time you will learn how your audience responds and it will guide your email marketing decisions in the future.

Alternately, if your list is big enough, you can take two test groups of 10K names each. Send your 'A' version to one group and your 'B' version to the other group. Compare the results and you could have a clear winner. Even a marginal winner helps you.

Then release the winning version to your full list and take the benefits of the best performing message. This only works if your list is large enough. You could do it with 500 names in each test, but the stats could mislead you. (A statistician can tell you why.)

Now on to the fun part.

ABT (ALWAYS BE TESTING) – 10 TESTING IDEAS

What the heck can you test? Here are 10 things to test in your emails.

1. **Subject lines.** Make them completely different or change one word.

2. **Body copy.** Write two different messages. See which compels people the best.

3. **Body copy length.** Settle the battle of long copy vs short copy once and for all on your own audience.

4. **Email layout.** Test two columns against one column, big header vs small header, alternate formats. Make your designer crazy.

5. **Time and Day of the Week.** Compare 6 a.m. to 6 p.m. on Tuesday. Compare Tuesday a.m. to Sunday a.m. Don't assume anything.

6. **Segments.** Test your target audience and see if you can zone in on a winning group. Better targeting equals better results.

7. **Your Call to Action.** Test text versus buttons. Test location and frequency of buttons. Compare alternate text in your link.

8. **Testimonials.** Add testimonials to the message and look for a lift.

9. **Personalization.** Go beyond *Dear Mitch*. Test personalizing other content in the message itself.

10. **Images.** Test with and without images (you might be surprised) and test competing images.

If you just take ideas from this list, you've got 6 months of ideas to run A/B split tests to make improvements. The biggest difference I've seen as a result of split testing is a 12-times difference. That can be HUGE!

CHAPTER 10

AUTORESPONDERS/DRIP CAMPAIGNS/WORKFLOWS

DON'T RUN AUTORESPONDERS LIKE THIS

You might have heard of an autoresponder by another name. Sometimes it's called an autoresponder, or the follow-up emails might be called a drip campaign or lead nurturing, but they all are capable of doing the same thing.

They take a stranger and start to build a relationship of trust. To what end? Simple, if you are easier to trust, you are easier to do business with.

Here's How You Design an Autoresponder Series for Maximum Effect

In order for someone to get to know you and therefore trust you, you'll want to step back from this project and answer the oldest marketing question in the book.

WIIFM?

"What's In It For Me?" Because that's what your reader will be thinking every time they open an email you send them.

If you plan to send 7 in a row, you'll need to be prepared to step up and answer that question for every email.

Or put another way. You have to give before you get. This act of selflessness shows the type of business you are.

It shows you have expertise and the confidence to share it to help others.

Once you have this part of the autoresponder messages down right, you need to make sure that every single message has an actionable call to action. It's only by having a call to action that, as a marketer, you can count how effective your messaging is AND take people one step closer to being a customer (if lead generation is your goal).

These two components TOGETHER make autoresponders work. My call to action is to have you read my latest blog post.

Autoresponders the Wrong Way

Day 1: Hi. Buy my product.

Day 2: Hi. Buy my product.

Day 3: Hi. Buy my product.

Day 4: Hi. Buy my product.

Day 5: Hi. Buy my product!

Day 6: Hi. Buy my product!!

Day 7: Hi. Buy my product!!!

Autoresponders the right way

Day 1: Thanks for requesting our free report.

Day 2: Did you get a chance to read our report yet? Chapter 2 is timely.

Day 3: Here's a resource you can use to increase your ROI.

Day 4: Has this ever happened to you? (story about lost opportunity)

Day 5: Here's a short case study about our most successful client.

Day 6: We've been very fortunate to receive these awards.

Day 7: Here's a checklist you can use to evaluate products like ours.

You think I jest. But when people learn about autoresponders they go about it the wrong way faster than you can say whateveryoucansayfast.

Seriously. How much better will a new prospect feel about you if they are on the receiving end of autoresponders done the right way?

What should trigger your autoresponder?

I often take for granted that certain styles and methods work with autoresponders and other styles and methods often have the opposite effect.

Firstly, it should go without saying, using autoresponders can give you an advantage over your competition right away. Most companies and professionals don't use them.

The simple fact of using autoresponders will set you apart from the pack.

But if you are going to use them, here are 5 examples of autoresponder sequences you should try.

Remember, you can use more than one autoresponder in your marketing. You could have a series for new newsletter subscribers and a different one for new customers. You can create an automatic series for any event that happens in your business.

Two quick tips.

1. Don't refer to anything that is time, date, or seasonal in nature. Your message 1 could go out next Tuesday (spring as I write this) or in 6 months (which would be in the dead of winter) so if you refer to something that's time related your message may sound odd.

2. Send the message from a person and make a personal connection. The more personal the connection, the more impact the email will have.

Here are a few examples of exactly how to lay out your autoresponder campaign.

1. **Use your top 5 customer service questions.** This one is pretty straightforward. Simply take the top 5 questions you get from your customer service calls and create a standard answer for each. Then craft your autoresponder series and frame it with, "Here are a few of the questions we get from our best customers." I'd still use a call to action in each one to see which ones perform the best. Space them out by 5 to 7 days apart.

2. **Outline your best features.** Frequency works in your favor in marketing and the same is true here. In each message set the tone with a "Thought you'd like to know..." and then describe one of your best features (complete with benefits). Again, space these 5 to 7 days apart and keep going as long as you like. These work best when you take the approach that you have to give before you get. Don't sell too hard in these emails.

3. **Educate them on how to get the most from your product or service.** Consider these messages part of your new customer orientation or training program. You'll be able to

show your readers that you care how they are doing and build a stronger relationship with them. Funny thing is, they will be more loyal to you when it's time for promotions to come their way.

4. **Lead up to a survey.** This option can be included in any of the first three or on its own. Doing a survey sends a message that you care. So not only do you send a powerful marketing message, but you will also be collecting data from your subscribers that you can use. This has been a powerful tool for me in the past.

5. **Lead up to a coupon.** You may have used an incentive (like a coupon) in order to entice people to join your list and you can send more than one message and more than one coupon to encourage repeat orders. You may have certain specials you can use, and for this series you are saying, "We enticed you with a coupon offer and here are a few others you might want to take advantage of."

If there is one thing you take away from this article, it's that autoresponders are not often used and that the emphasis should be on what you could GIVE your readers that will encourage them to be loyal to you.

It makes a big difference in your business.

4 REASONS YOUR AUTORESPONDERS ARE NOT WORKING

Email drip campaigns, or autoresponder sequences, or trigger emails are all ways of describing a series of emails that are sent over a period of time. These emails are triggered by a specific event, typically a purchase, or opting into a list. Some examples of email drip campaigns could be:

- A welcome series after your first purchase
- A 7-day course delivered by email

- Weekly tips delivered by email
- Training tips sent at specific intervals

These types of email series can be very effective in helping your business.

4 Reasons Your Email Drip Campaigns Are Failing

You create a drip campaign for a reason. And often that reason is ignored as soon as you set up the campaign and start to create the emails. After a while, you forget about the series.

Here's where you're probably going wrong:

1. No relationship is planned

In order for your email drip campaign to work you have to consider the relationship. Like any good relationship, there is give and take. Think about what this relationship is going to be like.

Yes, we know you'll be sending emails but what do YOU think they will do when they receive them? Will they be tired of you? Will they look forward to receiving your email? Will they want to take the action you want them to take?

Think this through BEFORE you start to design your campaign.

2. You are pitching your product right away

The BIGGEST mistake I see is the desire to pitch product right away. The series goes like this...

> "Buy my product!" "Buy my product!" "Buy my product!" "Buy my product!" "Buy my product!" "Buy my product!" "Buy my product!" "Buy my product!" "Buy my product!"

After a few of those, your readers know what to expect from you and it doesn't take them long to realize that's all you have to offer. Soon they unsubscribe because they know where to find you when they want to. As if.

3. You don't give

The best marketing advice I got about these email series is that you have to give before you get.

What can you send your readers that they will appreciate you for? What can you GIVE them? What will they think is relevant to why they signed up. What do they value? What can you offer they can't get elsewhere?

Start thinking like this and your subscribers will be very responsive to your emails... because they are worth it.

4. You're too impatient

See point #3. If you do give, you are in a rush to get. You want to see results yesterday... as we all do. Relationship building can take time. Trust can take time. I read a study recently that stated if you build a

solid welcome series of emails, your readers reward you with higher clicks and opens for your future mailings. I totally agree.

Here are some pointers to make the best email drip campaigns you can:

- Start with a Welcome message that is sent immediately. Show your appreciation.

- Send the series personally. Show you are real and care. (see above)

- Make sure your series is not connected to an event, season, date, or time. A proper drip campaign could go out in January, July, or September and the reader would never know you didn't write it personally.

- Run a survey. Just asking for feedback shows you are helpful and interested.
- Send a special coupon.
- Offer a customer service tip or "how-to."
- Tell a story about how customers are successful with your products/services.
- Test out different time sequences. One every day. One every 3 days. One every week. You'll see when you send too many.
- Keep each message focused on ONE idea.
- If you're going to send them a newsletter, let them know.
- Be real.

You can spend a lot of time trying to build a killer, winning email drip campaign right out of the gate... OR you can do what the professionals do. Create a good starter series and watch your statistics to see what your readers do with your messages.

Do they open them all at the same rate? Do they open the first one and ignore the rest? Does your open rate drop over time (most common)?

Once you have some data, you can go back to the drawing board. Recently a client and I introduced a new email (one linking to an exciting video) in the middle of their series. We didn't know how it would behave but we wanted to prop up a sagging middle bit.

We were actually a bit surprised to see a SPIKE in interest. This video was exactly the right message and the right medium at the right time. It's okay to test and tweak your series once you have it to get better results.

If you're using the drip campaigns effectively, you'll have more than one to work on and improve.

4 AUTORESPONDER STYLES

If you're looking for ideas on how to structure an autoresponder series, here are 4 styles you can model and build into your campaigns.

1) Follow-up to a lead (from stranger to friend and from friend to customer)

Seth Godin, in one of his early books, ***Permission Marketing***, talked about moving people, not through a sales funnel, but through relationship stages.

When you're creating your autoresponders think about how you can create a series of emails, which start to build a relationship. Remember the concept you have to give before you get.

Try 5 to 8 messages over a 45-day period. Don't do too many too fast. And don't do them too far apart so they forget about you. You're building a relationship.

2) Follow-up to a sale ('you did the right thing' with an upsell)

You make a sale. You have a new customer. Probably 9 out of 10 of your competitors stop there. Not you.

You're going to start sending an email here and there. You're going to send a few emails to cement the relationship. Think about how you will reinforce the sale.

Start with a customer service style message and expand the messaging to the bigger picture.

Finally, make sure you *make an offer*. This is where you think about the Commitment and Consistency side of human nature.

3) The story (leaked over time)

Everyone likes a good story arc. What's going to happen next? How will the story turn out? Share your story and let the reader look forward to the next email in the series.

I created an autoresponder sequence for a winery where we explained the history of the winery and how they evolved over the years to get to where they are today. There were challenges and triumphs and setbacks and big wins.

Each email also had a link to a wine related to the story.

4) Tips and more tips (52 messages)

This style of autoresponder is pretty simple. Create a simple tip each week. I had a list years ago of golfers interested in golf tips. Once they joined the list, there were 52 messages (and counting) in the queue.

The open rates were steady over the entire 52 messages although there were peaks and valleys as they found some topics more interesting than others.

In addition, every week, I would send an offer to the list. They opened the offers at the same rate they opened the informational autoresponders.

Is there a hints and tips sequence you could create for your readers that would keep them interested for a whole year?

SUMMARY

All right. Where do you stand? How do you feel about email marketing? Hopefully you have a new perspective on how to get more from your email campaigns.

There is no best way to use the teachings in this book. You can start at the beginning and implement what you read step-by-step, or you can skim and pick and choose which pieces help you at whatever stage you are at when you need it.

Successful email marketing is not 1 or 2 or 3 things done well (the home run) it is 101 little things done well (single after single).

My first sales manager used to tell me, "This is simple. It just isn't easy." I think email marketing is like that.

SELECT CASE STUDIES

LAKE STREET DIVE OPT-IN FORM

Today I'm going to be going through a little tip that teaches you how to make your sign-up process much more effective than it probably already is.

I discovered this new band, Lake Street Dive. I really like their music, so I zip over to their website to learn more about them. I like the website design. It's clean and simple. It's very elegant. It's powerful. Nice colors. Easy to read. I like that. And, you can notice right away, at the top right of the page, the first thing they've got is a "Join Email" list. I would probably put a benefit statement in here, and just tell people why they should join your list.

LAKE STREET DIVE FEATURED IN "ANOTHER DAY, ANOTHER TIME" ON SHOWTIME

JOIN E-MAIL LIST:

Subscribe

 A concert inspired by the Coen Brothers' film, 'Inside Llewyn Davis,' which is set in the 1960s Greenwich Village folk music scene, featuring live performances of the film's music, as well as songs from the early 1960s. Performers include the Avett Brothers, Joan Baez, Dave Rawlings Machine, Rhiannon Giddens,

ON TOUR

 Upcoming | Local Dates   Share:

I like the fact they used a "Subscribe" button instead of a "Submit" button. That's a good feature. And, I like the fact that they asked for email address only. The more info you ask for the less conversion you will get.

And, really, we're trying to get people to join our lists! I might give this list a special name and you'll see why in a minute.

main list

Almost finished...

We need to confirm your email address.

To complete the subscription process, please click the link in the email we just sent you.

Lake Street Dive
1055 Dean St Apt. 6
Brooklyn, NY 11216

Add us to your address book

« return to our website

Once I hit the "Subscribe" button, here is where I end up. You can see they're using MailChimp, and this is a generic, standard MailChimp page. This is typically called the "Thank You" page, which is where you get to after you hit the "Subscribe" button. People want to know if it worked.

Yes, it worked, and it gives you some instructions: "Almost finished. We need to confirm your email address" is what it says. What I would do is use more description here. I'd tell people more about what is going on. I would tell them what to expect. I would probably — if I'm going to add an incentive in — I would reference the incentive in here. "Once your email address is confirmed you will get access to...." something that you can only get by joining. I know that I'm expecting an email, so I hop to my email, and there it is! It comes from Lake Street Dive so it's whom I'm expecting it from.

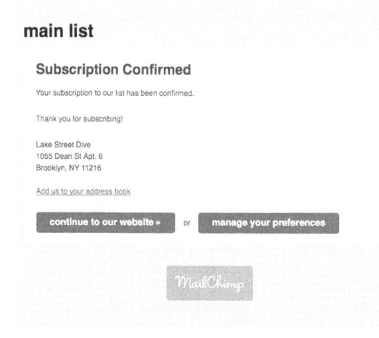

It's using the name of the list, called "Main List: Please Confirm Subscription". This looks like a pretty standard message. When I go into the email message, what do I see? Yep, it's a standard message. The name of the list is called "Main List". I would probably give this a better name than "Main List". I would probably rename this to something like "Insider Fan Club" or "Lake Street Dive Fan Club". Something more personal, secretive, and insider-ish so that fans feel like they are getting special treatment.

Next, I confirm my subscription... again, I would tell people why. I always tell people what to do and I tell them why. That always helps conversions. Next, I click on the "Subscribe me to list" and I go to the place I expect to be taken to. Again, this is a standard page.

This is typically called the "Confirmation" page, and it tells you that your subscription is confirmed. If I was giving an incentive, I might put a video here that would be only a video that you can get by joining the list. I might use that at the beginning, "Join our list and see a jam session from the club that you can only see by joining our list."

I would put something here that is kind of a cool incentive. I might give them a 25% off coupon. I might do something to incent people to get all the way through the process.

The three things I would do differently here are 1) to change the name of the list 2) make the information more descriptive and probably put an incentive in, and 3) to make a custom thank-you page and a custom confirmation page that actually are on the website. They would be on www.lakestreet-dive.com/thankyou. That's the page I would have people go to. Or www.lakestreetdive.com/confirmation. Instead of seeing this generic MailChimp page, people would be back on the website where they belong.

Follow these thoughts to make your sign-up process way more personal and way more effective.

The "take-away" you can take from this is make sure you go through your own sign-up process. Pretend you're an outsider, and just see what it feels like. Is it generic and bland? Is it personal? Is it customized? Is there an incentive in it, a promotion, something to seal the deal and get people through all of the steps?

The good news is your competition probably isn't doing this well, so you have an opportunity here, right away, to make a difference on what is often the very first engagement. If this was the first time I saw this band, and I interacted with their website, and it could be a better experience it would more likely lead me to maybe hit the "Buy" button and download some tracks, or download the music, or take a look at the upcoming tour dates. It would keep me a little more engaged than this standard off the shelf stuff.

CYCLING OPT-IN FORM PLACEMENT

This week we're going to do another cycling example. The Giro d'Italia is starting tomorrow and so I've been thinking about cycling. I trundle over to one of my favorite sites, a bike manufacturer, Trekbikes.com. I look around for someplace to sign up. I want to hear what's going on in the Trek world.

I have to scroll down to the bottom of the page to find something referring to email updates. It says, "Sign up for email updates and we'll deliver special offers and new product updates straight to your inbox."

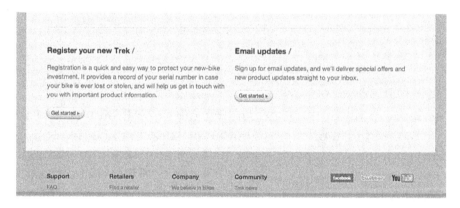

Not a great benefit, but they did use a Get Started button, not a Submit button.

Whenever possible you want to get the sign-up form or email update offer above the fold on your website.

Not just buried at the bottom like a last-minute thing.

Of all of the valuable things you can get a visitor to do, joining your list is probably one of the most important. Kind of above and beyond having them browse a few pages and then leave you forever. Keep that in mind. Try not to let your email updates offer hide at the bottom of the page, as so many people do.

I hit the Get Started button and connect with Trek and get great stuff. The copy here is just a little bit different. You can't see the whole page here, but they do have the real estate here to put whatever they want. I might put a few extra goodies here to really define or tell you why you should sign up. I would try to sell it a little bit.

Basically, I fill in the form and hit the Submit button, or I hit the button to get on the list, but before I do I notice something. The middle of the page, right underneath what you just saw, they have a secondary feature. It's the optional section and it says, "Tell us a little more about yourself so we can tailor our offerings to your interest."

This is really valuable. What's interesting about this is road biking and mountain biking people, there are some folks who do both, but they tend to be different camps. If you're a hardcore road biker, you tend to be that kind of person. If you're a hardcore mountain biker, you tend to be *that* kind of person. Yes, I do ride with people who do both. But, as an audience, if you're a road biker you want to hear about road biking stuff. You don't want to hear much about mountain biking stuff. If you don't have a preference, you'll just leave this be. For those people who do have a preference, it eliminates the irrelevant emails for things that aren't of interest to them. That's really a nice little feature.

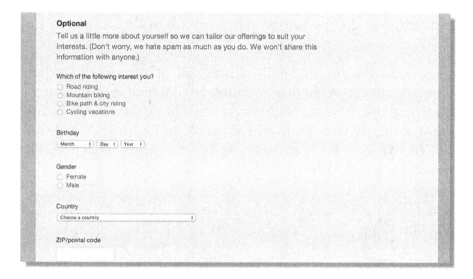

For the groups that checked cycling vacations, they just basically raised their hand and said, "Hey, I'm a person that's interested in cycling vacations."

Suddenly, they become a really targeted audience. Interestingly, they ask for birthday — presumably, they'll send a birthday wish. Gender — also interesting to ask for. Choose a Country — this is good to do so you know geographically where they are and, again, so you can keep things relevant to their audience.

This was a really nice feature that we don't see very often, but it allows you to start segmenting your audience right from the beginning. I like the fact that it's optional because remember the more you ask for the less you will get, in terms of conversions.

Then I get to the thank-you page. Thanks for your feedback and signing up. Interestingly enough I didn't provide any feedback, there was no room to do it. Right away they threw a curveball at me. Most of the time I'm not going to do anything different, but there's just going to be a little resistance in my brain.

It's going to leave me with a little bit of uncertainty when you're about to ask them something else. Which is immediately following up. It says, "For up-to-the-minute information and offers, connect with Trek on Facebook and Twitter." So, what they're trying to do is to basically build up their social media presence. Which is fine.

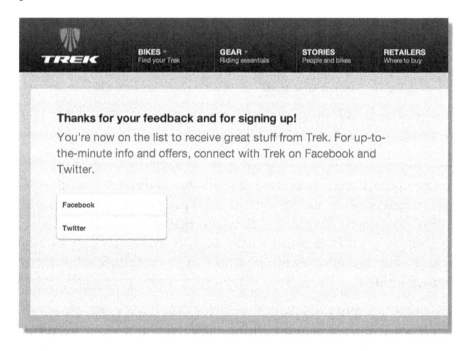

However, on a thank-you page, you have an opportunity to create a higher and better offer — a secondary offer. You completed the first step, the sign-up, and as a result of that you're could be to do something else. The thank-you page is where you can make that secondary offer. It might be a more valuable offer. It might be something, if you're an e-commerce provider it could be a place where you can offer people to buy something, like a new customer offer. It could be a survey.

There's all kinds of stuff you can do on this page. Most people just leave it lie at this. It's a good thing that they ask you to get to Facebook and/or Twitter. They're making an effort. Many people don't even use a thank-you page. This is just a reminder; make sure you use a formal and dedicated thank-you page. Personally, I think it should be personalized, it should have something on it that shows that there's a company with real people in it, not just a robotic webpage that flashes from space to space.

What did I notice then? I went to my inbox and waited, waited, waited. I didn't get anything. I didn't get a welcome message. I didn't get anything. I think this is a really big missed opportunity, big, big, big. The reason it's a missed opportunity is that the welcome message puts Trek in your inbox immediately.

What I like to do is tie the thank-you page to the inbox welcome message and let people know there's going to be a message in your inbox. It's going to be there immediately.

Go take a look at it. It could have a coupon, an offer, a special letter from the president, or a note from our sponsors.

There could be a million things you put in there. The important thing is don't stop at the thank-you page. This is your opportunity to begin the relationship. Don't leave me hanging until the next newsletter or the next piece of information comes out.

Start the communication and keep it going right away. This is often called the welcome message and is the first message in your auto-responder series.

The auto-responder series are the automatic messages that follow this one that start to build the relationship. Don't ignore those; they're really pretty valuable.

So what can you take away from this? Make it easy to find your sign-up form. Get it above the fold wherever possible. Don't stop at the thank-you page. Make sure you have a welcome email that happens right after that. I like the segmenting here. It's really good if you want to start segmenting. That's a good example of how to do it. Especially if you have lots of opportunities for people to do lots of things in different places. There are a couple examples of things done well and of course, like we always find opportunities to do things much, much better.

NHL EMAIL FAIL

Today we are going to do a rant. A rant is when I see something that is so bad it makes me crazy and this is one of those things. We're going to talk about your email campaign and your landing page and how the two of them work together. And how if you don't do it right it could cost you money, like maybe a million bucks, which is maybe what happened to this campaign.

Right now, it's NHL playoffs season. We're in the finals and we're in game six I think. I got this email a couple days ago. It got my attention.

This mistake is something that could be very, very expensive. I'll take you through step-by-step so you don't do the same thing.

Here I am, my email pops up and I see something that says, "Watch the Stanley Cup Final Live." That gets my attention. I don't have a satellite dish or cable. I do most everything on the web these days. Watching the Stanley Cup final live and on-demand in a web browser has got my attention.

Sort by Date ▾

Shop Your Way 5:09 PM
The perks don't stop: savings, swe...
Plus, In-Vehicle Pickup for ultimate
convenience | View online EARN &...

NHL GameCenter Live 5:04 PM
Watch the Stanley Cup Final with a...
Watch the Stanley Cup Final Live and
On-Demand View in Web Browser...

MYHABIT 4:02 PM
Up to 80% Off: Artwork, cookware,...
Free Shipping on orders over $99 in
the US EVENTS START AT 4PM PT...

JW Marriott Camelback In... 3:17 PM
Summer Pass Sale, Tournaments,...
Spend the Summer with Camelback
Golf Club! Sizzling Summer Pass...

I might want to watch a game before it's all over. I check into the email and this is what it looks like. It's a heavily graphic email and that's okay. The subject line says, "Watch the Stanley Cup Final with a Day Pass." It's very explanatory and gets my attention and that's something that I want. I'm interested. The top banner, where it says, "Watch the Stanley Cup Final Live and On Demand." *Live*, that's the right word. It says, "NHL GameCenter Live."

It's feeding me, it's taking me down the path. It says, "Don't Miss a Moment." **Okay, I'm sold.** It shows pictures of all these different devices. It definitely got my attention. Then it says, "Day Passes Available." The call to action follows up the subject line. It's nicely tied together. I'm hooked. Unless the price is crazy outrageous I'm reaching for my wallet.

Here's what happens when I get taken to the page. I click on the "Watch Now" button on the bottom. That's the call-to-action button. I click on that button expecting to sign up and get into the game center live. What is displayed to me is highlighted in red. It says, "NHL Game Center Live is no longer available for purchase this season." That is directly contradictory to everything I read in the email. I figure perhaps I'm not entirely smart enough. Maybe it's somewhere on this page.

I read everything that's on this page. There is no way for me to subscribe for a day pass. There's no word that says "Day Pass" on the page. The white box that is underneath that circled headline there that says, "No longer available for purchase this season," that white box says, "Classic games in the vault." I can go back and watch everything that has happened in the past — which is not what they offered me.

I'm stuck. I've been told I can get something and now I can't get it. This is the worst thing you can do, well not the worst thing but pretty darn close. Essentially it means that if this campaign went out to, how many people do we think might be on the NHL email list? I'm guessing we're talking millions of names on this list. These are hardcore hockey fans and they've been collecting them for years.

They just offered, I'll just make a guess, several million people a chance to watch live the playoffs, and we're in the playoffs. It's the perfect offer at the perfect time, but I can't get it. Dead in the water. Whatever people could have signed up didn't. The alternative would be to take them to a landing page here, and, instead of all of this copy that says I can't get what I've been promised, I would put it right there that says, "Live," "Day Pass," "Credit Card and Phone Number," "Sign Up Now," "Start Your Subscription," and "Get Going."

The call-to-action page has to match the email. Whatever people are expecting to see in that call-to-action page, you have to make sure it's there. You have to test. First of all, you have to set it up properly so that it runs, and then you have to test it before you send it out. This makes me crazy. The mistake is that it just wasn't thought through. These marketers thought that subscribers could find it on the site if we wanted it bad enough. Wrong attitude. Or, B, they just didn't test it before they sent it out. The landing page is sitting somewhere and never got used, which is a terrible crime.

Here's the summary: Follow the bread crumbs, the subject line, to the first part of the email, to the body copy of the email, to the call to action that all lines up. There's a suite of steps that take you through, step to step to step. When I send you to the next step you should be getting what I send you to get. Your expectations should be set, and I should meet your expectation. That's good email marketing.

Next thing you want to do is check your links. If you've got links check the links to the landing page. If I offer a day pass, you better have a landing page there that says, "Get Your Day Pass Right Here," "Sign Up for Your Day Pass," "Start Your Day Pass," or "Day Passes Now Available." I would do anything except say "Subscription Service is No Longer Available."

I would place a test order. Check your tracking, then you're ready to go.

A mistake like this makes you look bad and costs you money. How much money? I don't know, but it's certainly more than it would take to follow these steps. That's just what makes me crazy. A big company like the NHL might not miss a couple hundred thousand dollars here or there but if this is being done properly this adds up. If this is being done properly across the entire organization this is where email marketing makes a real difference. You do it properly, use it in all the right places.

In summary, hopefully this was helpful to you. I'm glad I got this off my chest.

AMAZON EMAIL FAIL

Today we're going to take a look at a transactional email sent out by Amazon, one of the top e-commerce and marketing companies in the world. However, in this case, somebody was not paying attention. I have to say, this is probably one of the worst emails I have ever received. As of this moment, it is the worst email I've ever received. I don't even have to think about it, after reading thousands and thousands of messages this one just takes the cake.

I'm going to take you through it step-by-step so you don't make mistakes like these on your messages. More importantly, so you don't copy what a big company does. Just because a large organization does their email in a particular way doesn't mean that either A) it works the best, or B) you should do it.

Let's take a look. This (on the following page) is the email I received. I started to read it. I put it here in a larger format in case you are able to see this on your screen. If not, I'll point out what it says and why they're good or not so good.

The very first thing I wanted you to know, this entire message is simply telling me I have a $1 credit. A $1 promotional credit. It's not something that's really, really, really exciting, but I got the message. The very first thing I noticed is the subject line. The subject line is not too bad. It says, "Your Amazon.com Promotional Credit." There's a little bit of curiosity there. I didn't know I was getting a promotional credit. Maybe it's something really good. I don't know at this point, I've got to go take a look.

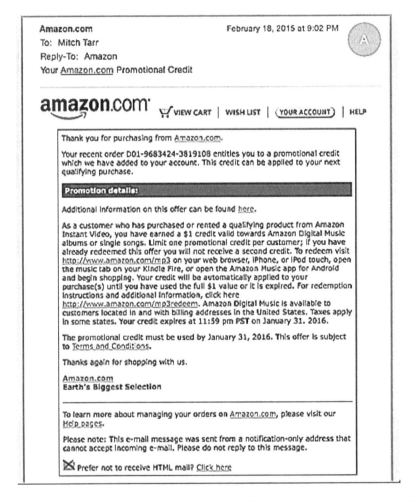

Now I'm in the email message and the first thing I see is the banner across the top. I think it's okay to have the Amazon.com logo there. Branding is good, although I know it's from Amazon. The very first thing it shows me is: View Cart, Wish List, Your Account, and Help bar. That starts me thinking right away. This is something different than a promotional credit. Maybe this is shopping or maybe this is even a piece of spam. Maybe this is something someone has copied and they're phishing Amazon and trying to make it something different than it is. Maybe this isn't even Amazon at all. Right now, I'm a little confused. I'm not quite sure what it is.

As I read through the message, this very first paragraph does a couple things. It says, "Thank you for purchasing from Amazon.com." Okay, fair enough. Then it gives me a recent order. It says, "Your Recent Order" and it has a 17-digit number which I can't connect or reference to anything. I don't know if I bought something, watched a video, downloaded some music, did something with my Amazon Prime account, or did something with my Amazon Associates account. I have no idea what this is. Right away I'm confused because I don't know what this is. The next thing that happens underneath this promotional detail — I'm starting to get a hint that it's a promotion — it says, "Additional information on this offer can be found here." It sends me out of the email right away.

At the very beginning, it's sending me confusion. I'm not quite sure what it is we're doing or what it's all about. Without having to read the whole thing, it's a dollar credit. I got a dollar credit that I can use in my Amazon account.

This entire middle block where the copy is jammed together without spaces, I like to have no more than three sentences in a paragraph in an email to make it easier to read. This looks like a big block of text and honestly when you read it is just plain confusing.

Here's a little sample of a piece of copy in the text, which doesn't even need to be there. If you see that copy on the right, that takes up two lines in the sentence and essentially tells me how to redeem my coupon. And it's complicated. It's not simple.

Typically, if someone wants you to redeem a coupon, they say "Click Here to Redeem Your Coupon" and you'll go there and figure it out. What's interesting is that there are nine links in these messages. Three of them are terms and conditions, three of them are questionably Amazon.com, and three are what I would call the call to action or the purpose of this email. However, they go to three different places, and only one of them mentions the promotional credit. The other two don't mention the promotional credit at all. This doesn't even make it easy for me to get my $1 promotional credit.

These are three different links that take me to three different places.

At the very bottom here, something else that this email has, it says, "Please note, this email message was sent from a notification-only address that does not accept incoming email. Please do not reply to this message."

You've heard me talk about this before, but the "do not reply" email message is a bad use of email technology. Maybe there is a different way they could notify you. If you did have a question, you did want to respond, you did want to engage with Amazon in some way that would reflect on their customer service this closes the door on that. It doesn't make it possible for you.

If you're sending any messages that are marketing-related or promotional-related, you want people to be able to reply to your message so that whatever question or obstacle they may have to doing what you want them to do is easy for them to get addressed. Then you're more likely to get what you want.

Let's just go through and summarize what you can do to not make an email as atrocious as this or as bad as this one.

Before you write your email have a clear purpose in mind. Is this a customer loyalty message? They want me to feel favorable towards Amazon.com. Is this a purchase message, they want me to buy something? Is this a try-a-new-service type of message? They want me to get involved in the music side and use their music service.

Before you create something like this, you really have to know why you are sending it. When you do write it, you have to be clear what it's all about. Like I said at the beginning, I had to read this a couple times to discover I had a $1 promotional credit waiting for me.

You can make your email pretty short. First thing, here's your $1 promotional credit. Second thing, how did I get it? You bought something from us. Third question, how do I use it? Click here to use it. That's really all this email has to say, and it doesn't take very much text to say that.

Ideally you'd like to have a single call to action, not two, three, or four different ones. If you're able to take people through the email message and it's clear, you're explaining what's in it for the reader, why they should click on the link then you want to have one single clear link to take people out of the email message onto your website. You can make this a button, a blue button that says, "Click here." You can make it a text link that says, "Click here," You can make it something even more powerful, like "Redeem your $1 credit now," and make that a clickable link — but don't have three or four different places you send people randomly.

The simple thing is, you start with the end in mind and work your way backwards before you start writing this message and making it really complicated and confusing.

If there's any one thing you can do just don't copy what you see big companies doing. It's not always a good practice. You don't know what's behind it. They might be testing something. There might be someone asleep at the wheel and definitely not monitoring email messages like this one, or it might be just a bad practice because they don't know any better. Being big doesn't necessarily mean you're really good at email marketing.

CHANGE UP THE USE OF EMAIL (WINERY EXAMPLE)

Today we're doing an email marketing review of a winery. It is a great review, or it's a great winery... it's both. So you're in for a treat today! Sit back, get your pen and paper handy to make some notes because there's some really good stuff in here, and I will just dive right into it. We do reviews like this every week. We generally don't know the company we're reviewing... we're looking at it from the outside in, so we also draw some assumptions. Quite often we can learn a few things by looking at how other people are applying email marketing strategies and tactics, and we can demonstrate ways to definitely make improvements, and you can learn from our observations and our recommendations. So let's jump right in!

First of all, we surfed www.stfranciswinery.com. A great winery just from looking at the website. It's a top-flight winery with a top-quality website. We really looked at it and said, "These guys are doing a great job." Then we started to look around and look at their email practices and said, "Wait a second, there are some things they could do differently that would definitely make a difference in their results."

The first concept I wanted to address today... you may have heard in marketing something called the "Average Lifetime Value of a Customer" — what a single customer is worth to you over their lifetime.

If a customer buys something from you today, then buys later this year, and again next year, over the next three years, they maybe spend five hundred dollars with you. The average lifetime value of a customer would be five hundred dollars for that time period.

There is a comparable measurement in email marketing which is what's the annual value of an email address. How much revenue does an email address actually contribute to your top line? For example, essentially what you do is you measure the email sales revenue and you divide it by the email addresses that generate that revenue.

For instance, if you are generating twenty thousand dollars a month directly from your email list, and you have five thousand names on your list, you would be looking at four dollars a month per email address in revenue.

Four dollars a month doesn't seem like much... depends on your business. Of course, over the course of a year four times twelve is forty-eight bucks — so for the purposes of today's discussion, I'm going to just round that up to fifty bucks and say the average annual value of an email address is fifty bucks a year.

If you have a list of five thousand names, five thousand times fifty bucks is your annual... what is that? Two hundred and fifty thousand a year in revenue directly attributed to your email.

This is something that you can calculate. First of all, you have to be able to track revenue that comes directly from your email. That's not terribly hard to do, but if you're not doing it, you definitely should be. Once you have that information then you can discover what an email address is worth to you on an annual basis.

For today's discussion, we're going to work with the figure of fifty bucks.

Every time you hear me say fifty bucks, that's from this calculation here. Twenty thousand a month coming from five thousand names, and we assume the list is flat... it doesn't get any bigger or smaller over the course of the year, which is not typical.

Back to stfranciswinery.com. Let's pretend we're searching around. We came across this winery, we want to learn more about them, and we land on their homepage. It looks like this.

It's shrunk down, so you can't quite see it, but there are a couple of really prominent things here.

Check out the main banner across the top where it says 2014 Zinfandel Producer of the Year. (And, yes, I caught the typo on that — so it's also a good thing to make sure that your website and everything is accurate, but that's not the point of this conversation.)

That's a rotating banner across the top and it cycles through all the great stuff that they do. It turns out that they have fantastic scores from Robert Parker. They're a fantastic place to hold a wedding. They have an excellent restaurant, voted number one by opentable.com, so it's really a top-flight winery.

When we first look at it we say, "This is fabulous. These guys are doing a great job." So the first thing we try and do is think… "I want to remember this winery. I want to keep in touch with them. I want to get on their newsletter list."

I start to look around and say, "Where can I do that?" And I'm only showing you the top half of their homepage. There's a whole bunch of more text underneath this that you have to scroll down to see. As you know, one of our best practices is we want to see an opt-in form or a sign-up form in the top half of the page — we want it to be visible.

Now the good news is they have one… you can't quite see it, which is the bad news, but the arrow really points to where it says join our mailing list and it has an email address and it has a Join button. Something they've done really well is by putting it in the header. This sign-up form is on every single page of the website. The bad news is, they're really just going through the motions. You can hardly see it… there isn't really a very good offer. It just says join or sign up for a mailing list. It's really kind of generic… there's no benefits in there… it's not very big… there's no flashing lights… there's nothing that points to it nothing that makes it stand out.

The good news is that it's on every page on their website. The bad news is that you can't really see it. So the first thing I would do is, I would make sure that I had a very prominent, boldly displayed sign-up option so that when you land on a page you can see it. Maybe you make the copy the same color as the logo. Maybe you make it bright red or bright green or something that's really going to stand out.

Maybe you make the font size big big big — so that's number one. Second thing is that I would put some kind of benefit statement on this sign-up form. What do you get by signing up? Is there something… some offer that they would make that would compel you to sign up? Something beyond just going through the motions of saying join our list or newsletter, which is what most people do.

The first step is to make your sign-up form prominent, make sure it's on every page, and make sure there's a benefit statement. What can you get for signing up? That's one thing that I would do that would definitely make a difference.

This is a very rich site. It's got lots and lots of content in it. Something else I would do — and this is just an aside — but I would also have a page called Join Our List, and if you had the real estate for it, I would put in the navigation bar across the top where I would have a separate dedicated button called Join Our List. And again, instead of "Join our list," I would put some benefit statement in it like "Get a ten-dollar coupon" or "Get free recipes" or just something more compelling than "Join our list."

That leads me into the second thing. Now, when we address this, we get the offers prominently displayed everywhere. I need a really good offer. I need something more compelling. Something that's great about this site is they are really rich in content, and they have a lot of talent.

When you go to the culinary tab, there are five or six options down there. One of the options in the culinary tab is a recipe section. Recipe sections are fairly common on winery websites and a lot of websites, as people see it as a value. Or "here's some additional content that will keep you on our site. We'll give you something for free and as a result you'll want to come back you'll read about the wine pairings that we match with these recipes, and ideally you'll want to order our wine to pair up with them not just somebody else's."

This is an example of "what if I wanted to do something completely different?" What if I wanted to really go after these fifty-dollar email addresses? What if I wanted more of them? If I'm getting a hundred emails a month now, what if I got a thousand a month? How will that change the nature of my business? At fifty dollars per email address, there really is a difference between picking up a hundred new ones a month or picking up a thousand new ones a month.

What I would do is... I would do something really radical... I would take the recipe section and hide it. I would make it invisible to the website people searching around, and I would make you sign up for it. I would make you give me an email address in exchange for our great recipes.

And why is that? If people perceive it to be valuable, it'll be valuable. If I give it to you for free, it's not perceived as valuable. If I make you sign up for it and leave an email address, it's going to have some perception as value... especially if I sell it a little bit.

Why are these recipes particularly good? Well... number-one-rated restaurant in the country... I would say that the chef behind that is doing a pretty good job. And I would want to get my hands on those recipes, because when I make them at home and I pair them with the wine, I can say, "You know this recipe, did you like it?" People love it, and when they say that, say, "Yeah, it's from the number 1 chef in the country at the St. Francis winery."

And if you have the St. Francis wine at the table at the same time, you have a fantastic story to tell. But you have to make these recipes valuable, and you make them valuable by making people have to submit an email address to get them. And when they submit an email address to get the first batch of recipes, you can also send them a recipe every month... every week to a couple of weeks... you can continually and constantly be in touch with them, and you can also send recipes a little bit in advance. Ahead of Thanksgiving, like a month before Thanksgiving, you might start to get the recipes going out... what can you do with turkey... and what wine and food pairings are going to go well with that... and, by the way, you can order some and have it in time for Thanksgiving.

Now you're starting to do marketing and all you've done is taken valuable information, made people sign up to get their hands on it... you've made a great offer, and you make this offer all over the website.

What would that look like? Make a banner that looks something like this:

We didn't spend any time writing, copy or doing any design on this, but this is the concept. This little ad should show up all over the website. You should basically pepper your website with your own banner ads... driving people to the sign-up page to get access to these recipes because they're valuable. Why? You tell people why!

Here's our offer — Join Our List and Get Recipes and Wine Pairings from our chef. Voted #1 Restaurant in America by OpenTable.

So that's a pretty good credential, and then a big bold JOIN NOW button. You click on that. It takes you to the page. It reminds you... it tells you why you're signing up, and what's going to happen next.

Suddenly you've started... same amount of traffic, but you're filtering this traffic... driving it to this sign-up page. You're using an ad like this all over the site, and suddenly instead of getting a hundred emails a month, it's entirely possible that this would give you ten times as many sign-ups. And now you're getting a thousand email addresses a month at fifty bucks a year — that adds up.

Definitely something to think about. It's a pretty bold move, but you're now starting to do more aggressive marketing, because you recognize the value of email address to you and to your business. It's not just, "Oh I've got ten thousand of them." The perception there is, when you look at your list, "Oh I've got ten thousand names, email is plentiful. I have plenty of email addresses." So you don't value them at very much. But if you looked at your ten thousand names and said, "Yeah, but each one is worth fifty bucks a year to me. If I had twenty thousand, that's something definitely to talk about." That's why the value of email addresses is something to keep an eye on.

What else would I do? Let's go talk about Facebook, because Facebook is something. It really works well when it's integrated with the email stuff. So we went to their Facebook page again. They're doing a great job on the Facebook design and layout, and they've got thirty-three thousand fans, so they're definitely serious about it. They're not fooling around. Let's just see some things we can do differently. One of the things I noticed right away is that there is a tab that says Enter Now, when I first go to the Facebook page, across the top I happen to notice that there's something behind it... maybe a contest.

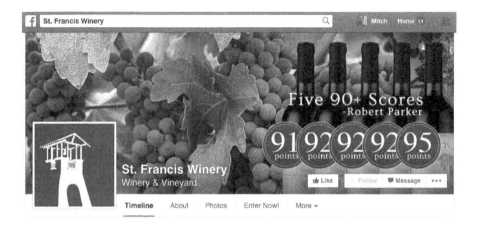

A part of the value of entering the contest is maybe you have to give up an email address, and that's starting to build the list. Let's just review a couple of little simple changes that the St. Francis winery can make to their Facebook page that will help them collect more email addresses. Why? Because at fifty dollars an email address, it's worth it.

One of the really simple things you can do is you look at your short description. This is in the left-hand column of your Facebook fan page. It's in the About section... it's usually at the top. And in this case, it says Wine Tasting/Wine and Food Pairings/Weddings/Private Events, and has a link to the winery — pretty standard issue. What I would do differently is, instead of having Wine Tasting/Wine and Food Pairings/Weddings/ Private Events, I might shorten that up a little bit, and underneath it I would put my offer.

What's my offer? It's the great one — get free recipes from our award-winning chef, and get a coupon for your first offer, and I would link to the sign-up page that's on the website. What I'm doing here is I'm taking Facebook traffic people that end up on the Facebook fan page. However they get there, that's a whole other story, and I'm directing them not to the website in general to let them kick around and see what there is to see — I'm giving them a specific and direct offer, and I'm sending them to that offer. Just that simple thing alone will get you more people on the list.

Now something else you can do — most sites you'll see on the Facebook fan page have apps. In the apps here, we see that there are three of them. One of them is the Enter Now, so there's the contest thing that we saw before. There is a Join Our Mailing List letter highlighted with the arrow, and there's a Pinterest app so we see that the social media connected up again.

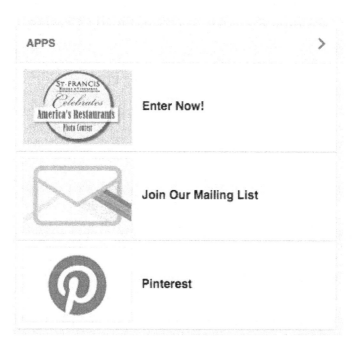

When I click on the Join Our Mailing List, I'm taken to a page still on Facebook, and it allows me to fill in the form and sign up for the mailing list.

Again, this is a vanilla cookie-cutter going-through-the-motions type of an offer. What if instead of Join Our Mailing List, you said Get Award-Winning Recipes, or Get a $10 Off Coupon? Make some offer that motivates me to go to that page, and when I get to that page put some copy in there that sells me... convinces me, shows me, demonstrates to me, gives me some benefits for being on the list.

What am I going to get by being on the list? It's way more compelling than just Join Our Mailing List. These days, join our newsletter, join our mailing list, and sign up here, are almost invisible to people because you see them a lot of places. They're not very compelling. They don't catch your attention. They don't tell you what you are going to get by signing up. What if you were to replace that Join Our Mailing List with one of these two different labels — Get Award-Winning Recipes, Get a $10 Off Coupon? Do you think that more people will go there because that's a better offer? So take your best offer, and put it there instead of Join Our Mailing List.

Something else you might notice, we can do this as well, where it says Enter Now what if it said there get a $10 off coupon? How many more people would click on it than if it wasn't there, or how many more people would click on it if said get our award-winning recipes? So just think about this when you get a great offer. Put your offer not only on your own website... put it on your complimentary surrounding sites, social media, and other places.

Make sure your offer is out there. If it's a great offer and it's proven to convert, there's absolutely nothing wrong with spending some money to advertise that offer. You can advertise it on Google pay-per-click. You can advertise it on

Bing pay-per-click. You can advertise it within Facebook paid advertising. There are lots of places to do paid advertising.

When you know the value of your email address, you know how much to spend before it becomes unprofitable. So you can make a determination. I'm willing to spend five dollars to get fifty dollars in revenue. I'm willing to spend ten dollars to get fifty dollars in revenue. I'm willing to spend one dollar to get fifty dollars in revenue per email address... but at least you know that number and you're making a good solid business decision, what your return on investment is.

If I told you that you could get fifty dollars in revenue for a dollar, how many dollars would you spend to do that? Would you do that all day long, as much and as often as you could, or would you say, "Well I don't know my margins are flat, that fifty dollars in revenue is not going to help me very much. I don't want it." I mean you might not want to spend a dollar on it, but on the other side of the coin, you might want to spend as many dollars as you could in order to get as many of those fifty-dollar email addresses as possible.

Here's what you can turn and take away from this case study. We really liked it once we got into it.

We thought it was a fantastic example to show you:

- How to know the value of your email addresses
- Calculate the average email revenue per year.
- Make a prominent offer all over your site. Make sure it can be seen. Make sure it's on every page.
- Make sure it's got a dedicated page.
- Make a valuable offer.
- Give people a good reason to join your list.

- Give at least a better reason than join our list, sign up for our newsletter... those things just don't cut it anymore.
- And finally, get Facebook working for you.

Get your email sign-up processes embedded in Facebook if you've got lots of traffic. Here's a tip — if you've got lots of likes, shares, and comments on your Facebook page, you can take your offer and put it right in your newsstream. Put it in there every day. Put it in there a couple days. Make two posts and one newsletter sign-up offer.

This is in addition to those little things that we talked about. If you don't have any action going on in your Facebook page, you can put these offers in all day long and nothing is going to happen... so this really depends on how your fan page is doing. But make sure you get your email offers out there... get them out there if it's a good offer. You know what it's worth to you. You have your R.O.I. calculated. You're way ahead of ninety percent of the people out that are doing marketing with their emails and on social media.

CHANGE UP YOUR OFFER (RECRUITER)

Today we're going to look at lead generation for recruiting companies. As per usual, we'll go out and do a web search, find a company, and I think we were looking for sales, sales rep recruiters when we came across Crawford Thomas.

It looked like a really good quality organization, so we thought, "Here's a great example of a single fundamental shift you can make in your lead generation philosophy that will incredibly change the number of leads that you get from your website." Incredibly might be a big word but just wait until you see what we're going to do here.

So first of all, we go to the homepage. This is where we find the beginnings of all websites information. And, typical banner, typical navigation bar, lots of good content on this page, really well designed.

As I scrolled down the page, however, I didn't really see anything that caught my attention. I scrolled and scrolled and reached the bottom of the page (this isn't typical user behavior, by the way — mostly they use the back button by now). At the very bottom of the page, I did find something interesting... a video.

It says Latest Video and it's labeled "How to have a great interview."

Here's where we saw a chance to make a small change that would have a big impact.

That video is just sitting there. Which of these two alternatives, regarding your intended audience, would most appeal to you?

Option A: They are interested and click on the video. Watch it. And leave your site.

Option B: They are interested, and fill in an email opt-in form to get access to the video. Watch it. And leave your site.

Hopefully you selected Option B. The visitor in Option B has demonstrated their interest by leaving you an email address in order to get at your good content. If it's good and relevant, people will have no trouble leaving an email address to get at it. If it's not good... well...

In this case, the target is candidates. What if I were interested in more clients? This simple change would get me more people to communicate with and keep in touch... and potentially turn into future clients. It all starts here.

You either have a missed opportunity or the beginning of a beautiful friendship.

Finally, step back and look at your website with a critical eye. The question you want to ask yourself is, "Where can I create an opportunity to trade an email address for something of value to my target audience?"

This is a great example of such an opportunity. A video buried at the bottom of the page.

FIN

.